A
Pregnancy For First
Time Parents

How to Be Stress-Free and Feel

Secure Throughout Your

Pregnancy Journey for Baby's

and Mom's Optimal Health

By

Harley Carr

entertainment purposes only. All effort has been executed to present accurate, up to date, reliable, complete information. No warranties of any kind are declared or implied. Readers acknowledge that the author is not engaging in the rendering of legal, financial, medical or professional advice. The content within this book has been derived from various sources. Please consult a licensed professional before attempting any techniques outlined in this book.

By reading this document, the reader agrees that under no circumstances is the author responsible for any losses, direct or indirect, that are incurred as a result of the use of the information contained within this document, including, but not limited to, errors, omissions, or inaccuracies.

Introduction

Pregnancy is an ongoing journey that can be full of first-time experiences for all parents alike. It is normal to feel unprepared and uneducated about the journey. If you have never gone through it before, or if you are just particularly nervous, finding out that you are pregnant can be a stressful experience whether you were trying to become pregnant or not. As parents, you are about to take on the responsibility of caring for another human life. It is natural to feel like you need all the help you can get. With the use of this guide, you are going to learn everything that you need to know about being a great parent. From maintaining a healthy pregnancy to having a relaxed delivery, there is plenty that you can do to ensure that having your baby can be the happiest and easiest experience possible.

Caring for a baby is a lot more than changing diapers and getting up throughout the night for feedings; it takes instinct and intuition. The only way to become great at this is to get rid of your fear and insecurity. Nobody knows what they are doing in the beginning, and that is okay. Remember that all parenting must start somewhere. Also, keep in mind that the level of difficulty you experience in your pregnancy does not indicate the level of difficulty you will face as a parent. All pregnancies are unique, and there are just certain aspects that you cannot control. Let go of this desire to control things, and fully experience your pregnancy.

You are a parent the moment you realize that you have life growing inside of you. Each choice that you make from that moment on is going to directly impact your baby. This is why your lifestyle plays such an important role in your pregnancy. There are plenty of people who realize that they are expecting, so they must change their lifestyle in order to accommodate a baby. This can mean anything from cutting down on spending to cutting down on partying. By using your common sense, you are going to allow your parental instincts to kick in. You know what is going to be best for your baby, so listen to these thoughts and feelings that develop.

Pregnancy has the ability to bring a couple closer together. While only one individual is going to be experiencing the pregnancy first-hand, you are both going through it together. Every decision that you make should be made with excellent communication and your baby's wellbeing in mind. This can often put stress on the relationship because so many important decisions must be made in only a few months. Know that it is okay to take some time to breathe before rushing into decisions. Discuss things openly with your partner, and try to be mindful of both opinions. Even though the father isn't going to be physically carrying the child, he is still going to have valuable insight into what he believes is best for the baby.

By learning steps that you can apply to your real life, you are going to feel comfortable and prepared for what is to come. Starting from the very beginning, you are going to learn how to care for your baby from inside the womb. Every mother should know what it means to be healthy during pregnancy, and that is exactly what you are going to learn. From finding out which foods you are able to eat to decide on how much exercise you can manage, all of these decisions are things that will impact your baby. If you are taking good care of yourself, then you are taking good care of your child.

As your pregnancy progresses, you will learn about the important signs and symptoms that all parents should be aware of. By discovering what is normal and what is abnormal, you will know when you need to seek medical attention and when you simply need an easy remedy. Pregnancy can cause you to feel things that you have never felt before, and this can be a scary experience. By taking away some of the fear, you will be able to have a better idea of how to handle these experiences and turn them into lessons. Not all pain is bad pain, but all pain can be managed if you know how to identify it.

Through delivery, having a guide that teaches you about what to expect is important because it will allow you to be more relaxed. A relaxed mother is thought to have a better labor and a higher chance of being able to deliver the baby naturally. While not all mothers can deliver this way, the guide is still going to be able to teach you techniques that will get you through your peak times of labor and allow for the safest possible delivery for your baby. Delivery preparation, no matter what kind of pregnancy you are having, is exactly what you will learn from this guide.

After birth, a different type of care will begin. You are going to learn the best ways to care for your newborn to ensure that they have a healthy start in their life. All of the decisions that you made before your baby was born will prepare you for the moment that you must start making them in-person. Much like pregnancy, parenting can also be full of trial and error. This is normal and expected, so make the most of the experience. Enjoy everything that you learn, and if you make a mistake, use that as an example of what not to do again in the future. Since no one is perfect, you should not have to put pressure on yourself to be society's idea of the "perfect" parent.

As a mother of three, I have experienced several different types of pregnancies. Beginning with my first-born son, the process was as smooth as can be. I had four-hour labor and was able to deliver naturally. It truly encouraged my abilities as a mother, as well as my ability to carry another child again in the future. Two years later, and my daughter was born. This pregnancy showed me the other side of being pregnant. From difficult symptoms to an emergency C-section delivery, I was shaken to my core. It was with the help of my partner, my midwife, and my resilience as a mother that I got through it and delivered a healthy baby.

Admittedly, this experience discouraged me from having more children. Though my partner and I wanted to have another baby, I was fearful that my next pregnancy would be as difficult as my last. Five years after our daughter was born, we found out that I was pregnant again. This was unplanned, but it automatically jump-started my adrenaline. It was a race to prepare for our third baby, and I hoped that my body would cooperate. My symptoms were difficult again, and finally, it came time for the delivery. Through meditation and breathing techniques that I had learned through the years, I powered through the pain. The labor was long and intense, but I didn't let this discourage me. I was able to give birth naturally once again, and although it was more difficult than my first, it allowed me to birth a healthy baby boy.

I learned that there is always going to be more to learn. No matter how prepared I thought I was there was always something to throw me for a loop. I learned how to love this aspect of pregnancy and parenting in general. Through letting go of my own unfair expectations of myself, I was able to just enjoy being a mom to my three children. And in doing so, my spouse was also able to do the same. When there are two people embarking on this journey together, it is so important that they are both on the same page. Through including my partner on my decisions throughout the pregnancy, we were able to form a great team and be great providers to our children.

The experiences that I've had in the last couple of decades have inspired me to write a guide that can help all expecting parents. While you might not be able to control exactly what goes on during your pregnancy, you can certainly do your best to make sure that you are prepared for anything. If there is one thing that I found to be important as a pregnant woman, it was the ability to expect the unexpected. Getting rid of all the imaginary standards I had about a symptom-free pregnancy with a quick and natural delivery allowed me to just enjoy everything that was happening to me. I saw each of my pregnancies as an important and valuable experience.

By reading this guide, you are going to be mastering the following experiences that many expecting parents are faced with:

- Noticing your pregnancy symptoms from the beginning and knowing when to take an at-home pregnancy test
- How to choose the right doctor for you
- What to expect and what questions to ask during your first prenatal checkup
- Deciding if any changes in your lifestyle that must be made after finding out you are pregnant
- Learning how rapidly your baby is growing inside the womb
- Learning about how your body is changing
- Knowing how to care for yourself if you get sick while being pregnant
- Caring for your skin if it begins to break out

- Dealing with your swollen feet and aching back
- How to properly nourish yourself through the nausea
- Becoming educated on how much coffee and wine you can drink
- Learning about how safe it is to eat fish and deli meat
- Deciding how long you will be able to work and knowing what maternity leave options your job provides
- Forming opinions on whether you'd like to have a gender reveal party or a 4-D ultrasound
- Traveling when you are pregnant
- Having sex while you are pregnant
- Determining how much you can work out
- Choosing your birthing option (water birth, home birth, traditional hospital birth, etc.)
- Knowing the signs of going into labor

All of the above topics will be covered in detail so you can feel as prepared as possible. No matter what kind of pregnancy you are experiencing, even if you are expecting more than one child, there will be a topic to answer your questions and find solutions for your problems. While most pregnancy guides only focus on the mother-to-be, this one will also include information that expecting fathers must know. By having both parents feeling as though they are prepared, the overall experience is going to be better and safer. There is no such thing as too much education when it comes to the topic of pregnancy. All of the knowledge that you gain during your pregnancy is going to be useful to you for the rest of your life.

After you are through reading this guide, you are going to feel informed and empowered. While there might be difficulties along the way, you are going to have all the tools you need in order to make the most of your pregnancy and deliver a healthy and happy baby. Regardless of how far along you are or even if you are simply considering having a baby, this guide is going to teach you everything you need to know. Many parents have utilized these methods over the last several years because they work so well. They will give you the confidence you need in order to be the very best parents you can be.

If you currently don't know what to do after finding out you are pregnant or finding out that you want to become pregnant, take the first step toward action by reading this guide. The sooner you are able to read this information and learn everything you need to know, the sooner you will feel ready to be a parent. Any questions you have, this book is going to not only answer, but also offer solutions. There will be no details spared as you navigate through each chapter of this guide. While there is no such thing as a perfect parent, there is such a thing as a perfectly prepared parent. This preparation truly pays off!

"Make preparations in advance. You will never have trouble if you are prepared for it." - Theodore Roosevelt

Chapter 1: What Are the Early Signs and Symptoms?

There is nothing to fear when you realize that you might be pregnant. While your body is about to undergo changes, accept that your body is going to know exactly what to do throughout your pregnancy. It is up to you to listen to these signs and symptoms in order to determine how to make yourself feel the best you can. Finding out you are pregnant can be one of the most exciting times in your life, so knowing how to read the signs are incredibly important. In this chapter, all of the symptoms you need to be aware of are going to be covered. From the ones you have probably heard of to other rarities, you will be very familiar with your body and what it is trying to tell you.

Most of the time, what you are experiencing is completely normal, even if you have never felt it before. Even as early as a few weeks into a pregnancy, many mothers agree that they were able to tell that something was different. If you have any sort of feeling like this, take a closer look at exactly what you are experiencing. Often, the symptoms in the very beginning can be so subtle that they are overlooked. It is only when looking back on these things do some realize that these were the pregnancy symptoms that they needed to be paying attention to.

The Most Common Early Signs and Symptoms

These are the classic symptoms of pregnancy that most women experience. While they might not experience these things at the exact same stage in their pregnancies, it is likely that they will at some point. Examine the following symptoms, and see how many you can resonate with:

- Missed Period: This one is pretty self-explanatory - a missed period is normally one of the earliest indications of pregnancy. When you become pregnant, you stop menstruating, so it is natural that a missed period would lead you to believe that you are pregnant. For some, this can be a misleading symptom because not all women have regulated periods. Some experience missed periods even when they are not pregnant, so keep this in mind. Compared to your normal menstruation schedule, determine if your missed period is a symptom or simply your period being sporadic. If you need further confirmation, you can consult your doctor.

- Tender and Swollen Breasts: Changes in your breasts are going to be felt early on in your pregnancy. This can feel similar to what you would experience right before you start your period. Not only will your breasts feel more tender and potentially even heavy, but they might also begin to change color around the areola and nipple. This happens because your progesterone levels are rising. You might notice this symptom as early as 1-2 weeks after conception. It will normally last for a while, often well into your first trimester of pregnancy.

- Nausea With or Without Vomiting: What most women picture when they find out they are pregnant is the rush to the toilet in order to vomit. Morning sickness is not a myth, but the way it is experienced among pregnant women can greatly vary. When you are pregnant, feeling nauseous is normal. This does not necessarily mean that you are going to vomit, though. Certain smells or sights can trigger this nausea, so pay attention to any moments where you are feeling this way.

- Increased Urination: Being pregnant puts a big strain on your bladder. As your baby grows and develops, your body must make room on the inside for this expansion. A fascinating process when you study it, all of your internal organs, even your ribcage, will expand or contract to make way for the growing baby. Since your baby is in your uterus, this happens to be very close to your bladder. This added pressure can cause you to urinate more frequently. If you notice that you feel the need to go more often, then this might be an indication that you are pregnant.

- Fatigue: Soon after conception, it is normal to feel a wave of tiredness crash over you. Certain tasks that are normally part of your daily routine can begin to feel draining. This is one of the symptoms that is commonly felt by nearly all pregnant women in the beginning. This also happens due to your progesterone levels increase. A spike in progesterone can make you feel very sleepy. Don't be alarmed if you feel like napping throughout the day because your body is simply trying to prepare itself for what is happening.

Whether you have all or one of the symptoms listed above, it can still be hard to determine if you truly are pregnant or not. By only listening to your body, you are solely operating on instinct. While it is great to try and predict this for yourself, the best way to find out if you really are pregnant happens after a visit to your doctor. Your doctor is going to be able to run the most accurate testing in order to confirm your pregnancy. While experiencing the symptoms can be exciting if you are trying to get pregnant, know that a visit to the doctor is always going to be the smartest thing for you to do.

Before you see your doctor, you can take an at-home pregnancy test. Most of the time, an at-home test is taken and then a doctor's appointment is scheduled soon after. A lot of tests that are available for purchase have increased accuracy ratings nowadays. Some even promise to give you results as early as five days after your missed period. Make sure that you keep in mind that no at-home test is going to be 100% accurate, but nonetheless, the process is still exciting. Seeing a positive reading is enough to change your entire life.

This is a very exciting time for a couple to go through together. A positive reading is when the idea of parenting becomes very real. Knowing that you are probably going to have a baby in less than a year's time is an incredibly special moment to share with your significant other. From that reading onward, you must come together as a team in order to do your best for your child. From visits to the doctor to picking out items for the nursery, you are both about to start this journey together.

Sometimes, you might have many symptoms of pregnancy, but find out that you are not pregnant. Do not let this discourage you if you are trying to get pregnant. Know that not every single mother got pregnant on the first try. Just as exciting as a positive pregnancy test reading can be, a negative reading can truly tear you down. Try not to let this hinder your desire to try again. Fertility takes a mixture of biology and luck. While there are ways that you can try to make yourself more fertile, know that you will become pregnant when the time is right.

Make sure that you are leaning on your significant other for support during this time. Whether you find out you are pregnant or you find out that it hasn't happened yet, you both need one another for support. This is a journey you are both taking, and while your partner might not be physically carrying the child, they are still a valid part of the entire process. Acknowledge this and express your appreciation often. Small things like this will keep a relationship strong.

Know that your pregnancy journey is not something that you have to share with the world right away. In fact, most couples do not announce a pregnancy until the end of the first trimester. This is usually for health reasons as well as privacy. Once a mother has reached the end of the third month, this is normally a sign of a healthy pregnancy. This also gives both parents the chance to decide who they would like to tell first and how they'd like to make the announcement. A lot of couples have been opting for gender reveal parties in order to break the news to their loved ones. No matter what you decide to do, take the first 13 weeks as your time to make these plans with your partner. Remember, there is no right or wrong way because this is your pregnancy.

A lot of new parents, especially mothers, feel pressure in the beginning to do what others are advising them. While certain tips and recommendations can be very helpful, know that you are the one who is going to be going through the pregnancy. Therefore, you have every right to deviate from "normal" plans and do what feels right. By listening to your symptoms and your body from the moment after conception, you are going to be on the right track to making the best decisions possible throughout your pregnancy and as a parent.

Less Obvious Signs and Symptoms

What most expecting mothers don't know is that there are several other symptoms of pregnancy that can occur during the first trimester that isn't as common as the ones that have been mentioned above. While these symptoms are not abnormal, you should be aware of them in order to understand what your body is going through. Some of these symptoms are less obvious because they are simply overlooked as normal daily functions. Make sure to be aware of these symptoms as well:

- Moodiness: When you are pregnant, you are going to experience a wide range of emotions. This can sometimes even occur over short spans of time. These feelings might cause you to believe you are unstable or overly emotional, but this is a normal pregnancy symptom. All of the hormones that are flooding through your body can cause you to feel moody. One minute you might be laughing with a friend, and the next you might feel like crying. This can be a rollercoaster of a symptom to experience.

- Bloating: We all feel bloated from time to time. It can happen after eating too much of a certain food, or just eating too much in general. There is also PMS which causes you to feel bloated sometimes. This is why bloating is often an overlooked pregnancy symptom. Thinking about it in the bigger picture, it seems obvious that bloating would be a symptom, but at the moment it can be easy to ignore. When you feel this way, it should feel exactly like the way that PMS bloating causes you to feel. It is the kind of pressure that doesn't go away even after eating an antacid.

- Light Spotting: Many women who are trying to get pregnant or trying to determine if they are pregnant see spotting as a bad sign. This usually means that your period is about to begin, or worse, that you are having a miscarriage. Know that light spotting is actually a normal and healthy pregnancy symptom. If you experience this, there is no need to panic. This bleeding is known as "implantation bleeding" and it actually happens because the fertilized egg is attaching to the lining of the uterus. This bleeding will usually occur about a week and a half to two weeks after conception. Around this time is when you would normally start your period.

- Cramping: As a woman, you are likely very used to the experience of abdominal cramping. Each month, cramping is one of the main symptoms that you will feel before you start your period. It is an indication that your uterus is beginning to shed its lining. Even when you become pregnant, this cramping can still occur because your uterus is working hard. Many expecting mothers say that they experienced mild cramping during the first trimester of their pregnancy.

- Constipation: Naturally, this is a symptom that can be easily overlooked because it is part of normal bodily function. Constipation can actually happen when you are pregnant due to hormones. This usually goes overlooked because anyone can experience constipation, some experience it regularly. The hormonal changes that you experience when you become pregnant can impact your digestive system, and this is why you can experience constipation. There does not necessarily have to be a change in diet to feel this way because the hormones are changing so rapidly.

- Food Aversions: When you become sickened at the thought of eating certain foods, it is likely that you are being impacted by the odor. Hormonal sensitivity is typically the reason for any food aversions you develop when you become pregnant. Any changes in appetite are usually overlooked because our tastes change constantly. You might decide that you are just being more picky than usual, but for a pregnant woman, there is a deeper reason behind it.

- Nasal Congestion: This is something that is hardly associated with pregnancy because it can seem entirely unrelated. Of course, feeling nasal congestion is going to lead you to believe that you are getting sick. This is typically something that you will try to treat with cold medicine or allergy medicine. When you become pregnant, your hormones and blood production can actually cause your nose to swell or dry out causing you to experience nosebleeds.

The same advice can be given if you notice these symptoms, much like the above symptoms. A visit to your doctor is still going to be the best way to confirm if you are truly pregnant. Being aware of your body is something you are going to become great at as soon as you suspect you are pregnant. Know that sometimes your body is just going through a lot of changes, so it is going to feel different. This feeling that you can't describe can drive you crazy if you let it. Your pregnancy symptoms are all normal, and you do not need to define each one in order to confirm this. Trust that your body knows what it is doing.

Talk to your partner about how you are feeling. This is the best way to gauge your symptoms. Though you know your body well, your partner is also going to be able to provide you with some additional input. Ask them if they notice anything different, and pay attention to even the smallest details. Most women who find out that they are pregnant agree that a lot of the signs were subtle or easily missed. A lot of women expect the symptoms to be way different than anything they have felt before, but they normally feel a lot like PMS symptoms.

In order to manage your symptoms, try to get as much rest as possible. A good night's sleep is highly underrated, and you are going to need a lot more of it the further along you get into your pregnancy. Also, make sure that you are eating properly. Well-balanced meals and plain foods are essential for any pregnant woman. On the days that nausea or food aversion is just too strong, you can opt for something simple, like plain bread or crackers. Getting something in your stomach is important, even when you don't feel like eating. Sleep and food are what fuel you. Hydration is also essential. Water is the very best thing for you to drink during your pregnancy. Since you are likely going to be feeling weak already, staying hydrated with water is going to replenish you.

If you need to leave the house for long periods at a time, keep in mind that you might be feeling your symptoms more than usual. Being on your feet for a while or moving around can intensify these things. Also, being out in public can lead you to encounter different scents that make you feel sick. Always be sure to bring a snack with you if you know you are going to be out for a while. If you are hit with a sudden bout of weakness or fatigue, you can get some quick nourishment by having a snack. Never travel without water on hand, either.

Ensure that you are taking a prenatal vitamin. This is going to keep your immune system and body strong as you begin your pregnancy journey. A great vitamin is one that includes plenty of B6, folic acid, iron, and calcium. Not only is this going to keep you strong, but it is also going to protect your developing baby. Allow your pregnancy symptoms to motivate you to stay healthy. If you start feeling bad, eating junk food and keeping an unbalanced sleep schedule isn't going to help. Think of your body as a safe home for your baby. Only bring good things into this home to ensure that your baby stays healthy.

Chapter 2: Healthy Options

There are many ways that you can ensure you are being healthy during your pregnancy. This does not only include eating plenty of fruits and vegetables. A pregnant woman has a lot to consider, and health should definitely become a priority. As the baby is growing, he/she is going to be receiving their nutrients directly from you. This means that anything you put into your body or do to your body will be felt by your baby. Providing you with the motivation to be healthier overall, it often takes a lifestyle change to make sure you are doing what is best for your baby and your health.

Healthy Eating Habits

As soon as you find out you are pregnant, you should be making all of the necessary changes in your lifestyle to maintain a diet that is healthy and nutritious. While the pregnancy cravings might be hard to avoid at times, your daily diet needs to be balanced and reasonable. Remember, you are eating for two, and anything that you eat is what your baby is also going to eat.

Pregnancy Diet

While there is no standardized diet that should be eaten during pregnancy, there are a few things you can do to become healthier. Typically, you will need to increase your caloric intake the further along you get into the pregnancy. In total, you will likely need to add around 300 extra calories to your regular diet. Aim to eat 2-4 servings of fruits each day and 4+ servings of vegetables. Carbs are actually essential to a pregnant woman. You are going to be receiving a lot of your energy from good carbs. Feel free to eat plenty of bread and grains. Protein is important, too. Eating meat, poultry, eggs, and beans will ease your fatigue and give you enough energy to get through your days. Since calcium is also a necessity, you should eat around 4 servings of dairy each day.

Daily Menu Sample

Breakfast: Oatmeal cereal with 1 sliced banana, 1 piece whole-wheat toast, 2tsp jam, 1 cup skim milk

Morning Snack: Yogurt and grapes

Lunch: Warm turkey sandwich with cheese on whole wheat bread, potato chips, 1 pear, 1 cup skim milk

Afternoon Snack: Raw veggies and dip

Dinner: 4-ounce chicken breast, 1 cup wild rice, 1 cup veggies, 1 cup skim milk

Nighttime Snack: Fresh fruit or yogurt

Seafood

A common question that comes up regarding pregnancy is if seafood is safe to eat. While the answer might surprise you, the FDA actually recommends that pregnant women eat more fish during their pregnancy. What is important is the kind of fish that is consumed. By eating fish, you are able to get a lot of valuable Omega-3 fatty acids and vitamins B12, B6, and D. These are all very important in a pregnant woman's diet. Fish that are known to be low in mercury and safest for pregnant women to eat are crawfish, Atlantic mackerel, salmon, sardines, scallops, shrimp, and tilapia. It is thought that a pregnant woman could eat around 36 ounces of fish each week.

In the past, it was thought that fish was entirely off-limits during pregnancy. Many women feared mercury poisoning, but through the newest research, you will find that certain fish are actually great for you to eat during your pregnancy. As long as your portions are monitored, you should be fine to eat fish as a source of protein. Some brands even take extra care to test their fish for safety in order to reassure pregnant women. Take a look around your local grocery store to see what your options are.

The fish that you need to avoid are bigeye tuna (common in sushi), king mackerel, marlin, and swordfish. These all contain high levels of mercury. Remember that eating fish during pregnancy should be a careful process, but you must also consider how much you are eating if you decide to breastfeed after the baby is born. While the baby is breastfeeding, they are still going to be receiving nutrition straight from you, so what you put into your body is still going to matter until they are weaned.

Nutrition

When you are eating healthy, your baby has a better chance for healthy brain development. Eating poor quality food is not only bad for your body, but it also limits your baby's ability to grow properly. Birth weight is important, too. When you are properly nourished during your pregnancy, you are more likely to give birth to a baby with a healthy weight. Once your baby is born, their birth weight becomes their first few months of development. This transition can be hard on a baby who is under-nourished and underweight.

If you are having a hard time with your pregnancy symptoms, your diet can help alleviate your pain. It can also help decrease your mood swings, improve your morning sickness, and give you easier labor and delivery. With all of the benefits that a good diet provides, it makes sense to prioritize it during your pregnancy. While you are naturally going to be gaining weight, you need to make sure that you are gaining the right kind of weight that will benefit your baby. Junk food might be satisfying every now and then, but it isn't going to support your baby's development in the way that healthier foods will.

Vitamins for You and Baby

As stated, taking vitamins when you find out you are pregnant is essential. While you can make sure that you are maintaining a healthy diet, you are still going to need an extra boost of vitamins and minerals to keep you feeling your best. Prenatal vitamins are designed for expectant women. They combine all of the essentials into one pill so you can ensure that you aren't missing anything. Not only do vitamins keep you healthy, but they also keep your immune system healthy. This is important because getting sick when you are pregnant can be a miserable and risky experience. If you aren't strong enough to fight the illness, it can begin to have negative impacts on your baby, as well.

Types of Prenatal Vitamins

Much like regular vitamins, prenatal vitamins usually come as pills or in a gummy. There are many different brands available on the market for you to choose from, so how can you determine which one is going to best suit your needs? Organic and vegan vitamins normally offer the best health benefits because they are not filled with any unnecessary low-quality fillers. These vitamins are only made with the best ingredients to ensure that you are getting exactly what you need from them. Normally made in a dry capsule instead of a gel capsule, it might be slightly more difficult for you to swallow. While gelatin makes for a smoother vitamin, it is an unnecessary animal byproduct that doesn't benefit your health.

If you want to stick with an organic or vegan vitamin, but you need something easier to swallow, look for veggie capsules. As they sound, the capsules are actually made from vegetables so they are easier to swallow and easier for you to digest, as well. If you choose, you can have your doctor write you a prescription for the vitamin that they believe is going to work best for you. While a prescription prenatal isn't mandatory, some women prefer this because they appreciate their doctor's opinion. If you decide to go with a more traditional, over-the-counter vitamin, make sure that you at least avoid the ones with added salts and synthetic materials. Doing some research on the top brands can help you make your decision.

Why is Vitamin D Important?

Technically speaking, Vitamin D is actually a steroid vitamin that supports your immune system, keeps your cell division healthy, and makes sure that your bones remain strong. These are all very important for people, in general, but especially for pregnant women. Most prenatal vitamins do not supply you with the recommended amount of vitamin D necessary to support your pregnancy. Try to find one that offers 4,000 IU of vitamin D each day, or else find a supplement that will give you the remainder of what you need.

Vitamin D can be absorbed by your body as well as taken in a pill form or through various foods. Know that sunshine and a glass of milk isn't going to be enough vitamin D for any pregnant woman. Ensuring that you are taking your prenatal each day, with or without a supplement, is going to protect you from cancers, autoimmune disorders, neurological issues, and cardiovascular diseases. The area in which you live also plays a role in how much vitamin D you need. If you are in an area that experiences little sunshine, then you might need to consult with your doctor to ensure that 4,000 IU of vitamin D daily is going to be enough during your pregnancy.

Natural Sources of Vitamin B6 and Why It Is Important

Another vitamin that is important to your baby's brain development and immune function is vitamin B6. Along with folic acid, which is necessary for developing your baby's neural tube in the early stages, vitamin B6 has been known as another essential vitamin for an expecting mother. Vitamin B6 helps with early development, and you will want to provide your baby with all the nutrients possible in the beginning. Another great benefit of taking vitamin B6 is that some studies have shown that it can reduce nausea and vomiting for pregnant women. Those who are particularly sensitive to these symptoms have found great relief by increasing their vitamin B6 intake. The recommended amount to take is around 1.9 milligrams per day. Unless otherwise prescribed by your doctor, you should not exceed 100 milligrams in a single day. While an overdose of vitamin B6 isn't going to be particularly dangerous, it will make you feel sick or lead you to experience indigestion if you aren't careful.

If you are looking for natural ways to get B6, eat plenty of chicken, salmon, potatoes, spinach, hazelnuts, bananas, cereals, and vegetable juice. These are all great foods to include in your pregnancy diet, and they will also benefit you by getting your B6 levels where they need to be. Getting enough B6 isn't hard if you are being mindful of it. As long as you are eating a well-balanced diet, it is likely that you are indeed getting the amount you need. Talk to your doctor if you are ever unsure if you need to add a supplement to your vitamin regimen. Each pregnant woman is going to have different needs. Even if you are taking the recommended amount, yet you still feel that you are weak or experiencing bad nausea, you can always talk to your doctor about increasing your dosage.

How to Treat Illness When Pregnant

Getting sick when you are pregnant can be a scary feeling. Not only are you going to be battling your illness, but you are also going to be worrying over your baby's health and development. It is no secret that a weakened immune system is not good for a growing baby during pregnancy, but there is no need to panic. We all get sick sometimes, no matter how careful we are. By taking extra precautions as an expecting mother, you will be able to combat your colds in no time.

Starting from the beginning, avoid situations that could potentially get you sick. For example, if you know that your friend is sick, do not spend time around them until they are feeling better. Limiting your exposure to other people and other germs is going to help your immune system tremendously. If you begin to feel your immune system crashing, get some probiotics into your body. These are live microorganisms that provide you with health benefits. They eat away at the bacteria and make you stronger and better able to maintain your health. You can either consume them in liquid form, pill form, or through certain foods such as yogurt. Probiotics have also been known to help your digestion, too.

Get plenty of rest, and take some time to incorporate physical activity into your daily routine. While you do not need to have a cardio-focused workout each time, you should still make sure that you are up and moving as much as possible without overworking yourself. While melatonin is a known sleep aid, it has not been proven safe to use while you are pregnant. Do your best to regulate your sleep schedule naturally by getting to bed at a decent hour, taking naps when necessary, and winding down before you are ready to go to bed.

One of the very best steps you can take to avoid getting sick is to wash your hands frequently. After you go out in public, wash your hands as soon as you can. Being around a lot of germs and bacteria is going to increase your chances of getting sick, so washing your hands a lot never hurts. Make sure that you use anti-bacterial wipes around the house on doorknobs, cabinet fixtures, the toilet flusher, and any other surfaces that are touched frequently.

What is Safe to Take?

If you do end up getting sick, you might need medicine to help you fully recover. Along with getting plenty of rest, staying hydrated, and taking your prenatal vitamins, you need to know which medicines are safe for you to take during your pregnancy. If you are in pain, acetaminophen (Tylenol) is a known drug that is safe to take. While most doctors recommend avoiding ibuprofen (Advil or Motrin) during the third trimester, it is safe to take in moderation during the first two trimesters if necessary.

54

These drugs have been tested by the FDA in terms of how safe they are for pregnant women to take. But the safest pain reliever by far is acetaminophen. Aspirin should be avoided at all costs; it is known to be among the most harmful to an expecting mother.

If you are experiencing a cold, it is suggested that you avoid taking any cold medicine until you are at least 12 weeks along. This is to minimize any risks that are to be experienced. If you must take cold medicine, some safe options for you are Vicks, Robitussin, cough expectorant (day), and a cough suppressant (night). While Sudafed is another popular cold medicine, it has actually not been tested by the FDA for safety during pregnancy. If you'd like to take Sudafed for your cold, consult with your doctor first.

Heartburn and indigestion are something that pregnant women experience often. Sometimes, these symptoms get so bad that the mother needs to regularly take medicine in order to alleviate the pain. Over-the-counter antacids are almost always safe to take. Look for ones that contain magnesium, calcium, aluminum, and alginic acid. Some examples include Tums, Mylanta, Pepcid, and Maalox. If the heartburn is more severe, you might need to discuss some other options with your doctor. Zantac and Tagamet are two that are known to be prescribed by doctors to pregnant women.

Allergies can make your pregnancy very difficult. They cause you to feel sick without actually experiencing a cold. If you need some allergy relief during your pregnancy, you can safely take Benadryl, Claritin, Alavert, Zyrtec, and Chlor-Trimeton. These are considered safe for any light to mild allergy sufferers. If your allergies are too much for any of these medications to handle, ask your doctor is you can take Rhinocort, Flonase, and Nasonex. The summer months can cause your allergies to become more severe because of all the pollen floating around. Keeping your house clean and your windows closed can help limit your exposure to these allergens.

As mentioned, constipation is an often overlooked symptom of pregnancy. While you are normally going to be able to let it pass on its own, there are times when you could benefit from some medicine to help you stay comfortable. Stool softeners and laxatives are mainly known for being safe during pregnancy, but this is something you should consult your doctor before taking one. If drinking more water and adding more fiber to your diet doesn't provide enough relief, you can ask your doctor about taking Colace, Surfak, Dulcolax, or Senokot.

Chapter 3: What is Safe and What is Not?

Finding out you are pregnant can change a lot in your life. Aside from preparing for the arrival of your new baby, you must also ensure that your old habits do not create conflict with your desire to have a healthy pregnancy. By becoming smarter and more aware of the dangers of the things you might already do, you are going to be protecting your baby from the very beginning. While there are some things you might need to give up, you should never feel ashamed. A lot of parents, both mothers, and fathers alike find that the pregnancy stage is when they were most motivated to make lifestyle changes. Keeping your baby in mind, consider if anything you are currently doing is going to be dangerous or harmful to your baby's development.

In this chapter, you will learn how to give up your vices by replacing them with healthier options. Once you have mastered this willpower, you are going to feel rightfully proud of your accomplishments. Through becoming better at doing research and reading labels carefully, you are going to be able to spot dangers to your health and to your baby's health before being told by your doctor. Then, you are going to learn how to listen to your body and know when it is the right time to give yourself the necessary rest and relaxation. While there are plenty of places to go and things to do, know that pregnancy is going to temporarily limit these for you. In the end, it is all going to be worth it as you have a successful pregnancy and an effortless delivery to a healthy baby.

Caffeine, Alcohol, and Tobacco

Drinking coffee, consuming alcohol, and smoking tobacco are the top 3 most common vices that anybody can have. After finding out you are pregnant, if you participate in any of these things, then you must make some immediate changes in order to ensure that your baby is protected from these actions. If you cannot get through your day without a cup of coffee, the good news is that you don't have to when you are pregnant! It is actually okay for a pregnant woman to drink around 200mg of caffeine each day - that is about 2 cups. A common myth that has been circulated for years is that you must give up coffee as soon as you find out that you are pregnant. While you don't want to overdo it, as long as you are monitoring your intake, caffeine is actually not going to be harmful to your baby.

Alcohol, on the other hand, has very negative impacts on the health of a pregnancy and even on the health of your baby if you drink while you are still breastfeeding. Because all that you consume is going directly to your baby, even a single drink is going to be impacting your child. The alcohol will cross from the bloodstream into the placenta, and your baby will have no choice but to consume it as well. This can lead to many damaging long-term effects such as learning disorders, malformation of the heart, damage to other organs, and birth defects. If you are trying to become pregnant, it is best to give up alcohol before conception. This can be a tough habit to kick, but it will terribly damage your baby's health if you end up drinking while pregnant or breastfeeding.

Understandably, smoking is a common coping mechanism for stress. It is very easy to become addicted to tobacco products, and when you become pregnant, quitting can be a nightmare. Quitting anything cold turkey is going to cause you to experience withdrawal symptoms, so quit before you become pregnant if you can help it. Cigarettes are filled with toxins that are going to enter your baby's bloodstream the same way that alcohol will. Nicotine of any kind is extremely harmful to your baby, and it can narrow the umbilical cord. This can mean that your baby's oxygen supply is reduced. Simply smoking less isn't going to be a healthy option during your pregnancy; you must kick the habit entirely. If you cannot give up smoking, then you need to evaluate your desire to become a parent. Your baby's health must come before any coping mechanisms or vices that you are holding on to.

Surviving Pregnancy without Vices

Though getting rid of your vices is going to be a difficult process, it is one that is worth every second. Think about how much healthier your baby is going to be when you can lead a healthy lifestyle. Your lifestyle not only matters during your pregnancy but before and after it as well. Starting by cutting down on your coffee intake, you can then find other ways to gain energy throughout the day. Changing the way you eat is one way to accomplish this. If you eat several small meals throughout the day instead of 3 big ones, you are going to have more energy distributed throughout your body at any given time. For a pregnant mother, having extra energy is very important. Exercise can also give you a boost in energy. While it might make you tired at the moment, the endorphins that you feel afterward are enough to keep you going.

Practicing yoga can be a great way to assist you with quitting cigarettes. If you are trying to get pregnant, begin taking yoga classes right away to assist with your breathing. Yoga is helpful for quitting smoking because it teaches you other ways to breathe deeply without needing to rely on nicotine. If you are able to quit smoking for the duration of your pregnancy, there is no need for you to pick up another cigarette again. These eight to nine months that you spend smoke-free should show you how great you can feel without having to rely on this vice. Not to mention, secondhand smoke is extremely harmful to babies and children. You wouldn't want to pick up a cigarette immediately after you give birth because your baby is still going to feel its impacts by being around you.

Drinking alcohol is normally picked up as a social habit. A lot of people enjoy having a drink with friends as a form of relaxation and a way to unwind. As you know, excessive alcohol consumption is terrible for your liver and heart. When you are pregnant, if you drink, all of these negative impacts are going to be passed straight down to your baby. If you would still like to experience the fun of going out without drinking, you can feel free to hang out with your friends as much as you want. Order seltzer water so you can still have something to sip on without drinking alcohol. Sometimes, the feeling of having a drink in your hand can be enough to supplement the fact that you aren't drinking.

Why You Must Beware of Deli Meats

Many pregnant women believe that they need to avoid eating deli meat. A lot of these meats are filled with nitrates and additives that are harmful in general. They are high in saturated fats and sodium, which need to be consumed in moderation while you are pregnant. If you decide to eat deli meat, you must make sure that it is properly stored and heated up to 165°F. There are 3 basic types of deli meat: whole cuts that are cooked and sliced, reconstructed pieces of several different types of meat that are put together, and processed meat. You should only eat the first type of deli meat because it is going to be least harmful to you.

Understandably, cravings happen while you are pregnant. You might get intense cravings to eat deli meat, and this is okay, as long as you are mindful of its quality. The following are the safest to eat during your pregnancy:

- Turkey Breast: This is a low-calorie option with a lot of protein. Turkey can help to lower your cholesterol and blood sugar.
- Deli Sliced Ham: It is another protein-packed option that also provides you with plenty of calories. Ham sandwiches with lettuce are great to eat to satisfy your deli meat craving.

- Chicken Breast: This is the healthiest option for you to consume during your pregnancy. It is actually recommended that you eat plenty of chicken breasts in order to keep a balanced diet.
- Grilled Pork Slices: Pork is something that will keep you satiated. It is more filling than a lot of other deli meat, and it is a great source of calcium and protein.

A general rule for what to avoid should be anything that is cured in salt. This is going to contain too much sodium, plus it is going to be filled with nitrates. If you consume too much salt during your pregnancy, you could experience hypertension and edema. Also, nitrates are carcinogenic. While a few bites of these meats won't be enough to create long-term impacts, you should definitely be opting for the healthier deli meat overall.

Much like fish, there is more of a misconception that you must not eat any deli meat at all. As long as you are eating it in moderation, you will be doing what you can to ensure you are being safe. The type of meat matters more than the frequency in which you decide to eat it. If you are ever unsure about the deli meat you are consuming, consult your doctor for a better recommendation to satisfy your craving.

Reading Content Labels

The easiest way to determine if something is safe for you to eat or use during your pregnancy is to become familiar with its content label. When you are looking at food labels, pay attention to the serving size. This is going to provide you with a guideline for how to read the contents. As you know, when you are pregnant, you need to increase your caloric intake. If something is high in calories, this does not necessarily mean that you need to avoid it. What you need to observe next is the amount of trans fat and saturated fat. These fats are the kind that isn't going to provide you with nutritional benefits.

Cholesterol comes from animal products. Small amounts of cholesterol are okay for pregnant women, but too much can lead to health problems. Much like cholesterol, sodium is also something that needs to be closely monitored. One teaspoon of salt is the recommended amount each day. Anything higher is going to lead to high blood pressure and cause you to remain bloated. Carbohydrates are generally good for you. When you eat plenty of bread and grains, you are going to be gaining energy while staying full. If you consume too much, then you are going to raise your blood glucose level.

As you know, fiber is great for pregnant women. If you are experiencing constipation, adding more fiber to your diet is going to be helpful. In order to determine if something has a healthy amount of fiber in it, start with foods that have more than five grams of fiber and subtract half from the total amount of carbohydrates. If you can aim for around 25-30 grams of fiber each day, you will be in a good range. Sugar must be eaten in moderation, but this is something that you can likely monitor if you are aware of what you are eating.

There isn't really such thing as eating too much protein when you are pregnant. Any protein that your body gets goes straight to your body and to your energy level. The better you feel, the better your baby is going to develop. It is thought that pregnant women who consume a lot of protein give birth to healthier babies with fewer illnesses in the future. As long as you can stay strong, then your baby is likely going to be strong as well.

Reading content labels does not have to be a complicated experience. As long as you know how to seek out the benefits you are looking for, you should not have a problem with determining which foods are going to benefit you during pregnancy. If you are ever unsure about whether or not it would be good to eat something, you can keep in mind the various ratios of its calories, carbohydrates, sodium, fiber, sugar, and protein to see if you would be receiving any nutritional value from consuming the specific food.

Traveling While Pregnant

Most pregnant women are able to travel safely until they reach the 36-week mark. The best time to travel is during your second trimester. Specifically, you should plan to travel when you are 14-28 weeks pregnant. This is because most of your symptoms should be manageable by this point, and you will not be too close to your due date. There are a few conditions that will limit your ability to travel, and these include preeclampsia, pre-labor rupture of membranes, and preterm labor. Also, if you are carrying more than one baby, this makes travel riskier. While you might have the urge to get away, as a pregnant woman, you will need to consider all of the potential risks involved.

In terms of where you can travel, you can go just about anywhere you want. The only areas that should definitely be avoided are those known for

Zika outbreaks. The Zika virus is very harmful to unborn babies, causing potential birth defects and developmental problems. Zika virus is spread by mosquitoes, and it is not the only disease they carry. Malaria should be another concern when you plan on traveling. To keep track of these dangerous areas, you can do some research online to see which countries are currently experiencing the viruses.

Before you go on any trip, it is a good idea to visit your doctor to make sure that everything is looking alright. Mention the trip and get an honest, professional opinion on whether or not your doctor believes you are suited to travel. Bring plenty of over-the-counter medications with you in order to treat your basic symptoms, and keep in mind when your due date is in case you do need to seek medical attention while away. Medical professionals are going to need to know what you are taking and when you are due in order to treat you. Ensure that you are up to date with your vaccines, and be cautious in general. Travel insurance is a good option to consider in case you are forced to cancel your trip for any reason relating to your pregnancy. Otherwise, you should still be able to experience the joys of traveling until getting closer to your due date.

When to Take Bed Rest

At a certain point in your pregnancy, it might benefit you to take bed rest. This is just as it sounds, and it is meant to alleviate your symptoms near the end of your pregnancy. Before you go into labor, symptoms can become intensified. The level of bed rest you need is going to depend on how much difficulty you are having. This can range from as simple as resting periodically in your own bed at home to becoming hospitalized and monitored for your safety. If this happens to you, know that many pregnant women go through periods of time where they must be on bed rest, too. It can become a normal part of your pregnancy journey.

Your doctor will usually be the one to tell you to take bed rest, but you also should be aware of the signs that you need it. These signs include vaginal bleeding, high blood pressure, premature labor, gestational diabetes, cervical effacement, poor fetal development, placenta complications, and history of pregnancy loss. Bed rest is meant to take the stress off your body so your baby can continue to grow at a healthy rate.

The main benefit of bed rest is simply that you get the chance to relax. When there is too much going on in your life, this can cause stress and complications in your pregnancy. Whether you are working too much or doing too much physical activity, bed rest gives your body the chance to reset. The best position for bed rest is being on your side with your knees bent and a pillow between them to make the position more comfortable. You can also rest on your back with a pillow to support your hips/legs so they are elevated above your shoulders. If you still feel discomfort while on bed rest, try squeezing stress balls and turning your wrists/feet in circles.

Chapter 4: Pregnancy Fears and Reasons Not to Worry

There are plenty of "what ifs" that will likely be running through your head as you enter your pregnancy journey. For all of the things that can go wrong, it can be difficult to reassure yourself that everything is going to be alright. Worrying is one of the main causes of illness, and if you can help it, you must do your best to set the worries aside in order to preserve your health. The following are some fears that many pregnant women encounter. As you will experience, there are always going to be solutions and options for you.

- Fear of Miscarrying: Statistically, less than 20% of pregnancies end in miscarriage. Once you have gotten past your first few weeks of pregnancy, then you are likely going to carry a healthy baby to term. Once your doctor can see and hear a heartbeat (at the 6-8 week mark), then your risk of miscarriage drops to below 5%.

- Being Too Sick: Many women worry that morning sickness takes away the nutrition that is supposed to be going to your baby. If you are going through a spell of frequent vomiting, as long as you are still taking your prenatal vitamins regularly, then your baby is still going to be getting nutrition. Do your best to eat smaller meals, more frequently, to ease the sickness. Babies have the ability to absorb nutrients very well, so even when you feel that you can't keep anything down; know that your baby is still eating.

- Worrying About Birth Defects: While your baby can be tested for all of the different birth defects that are known, it is still natural to worry that your baby is going to be born with one. The risk of having a baby with a birth defect, without any clear indicators, is only 4%. This statistic includes serious birth defects as well as small ones that can improve as the baby grows up.

Nausea and Morning Sickness

Feeling nauseous is one of the most common pregnancy symptoms that you will experience as a pregnant woman. Up to 70% of expecting mothers can identify with this feeling. Most nausea and morning sickness tends to occur during the earlier months of your pregnancy. Though it is common in your first trimester, sometimes, it can last longer. The exact link between nausea and pregnancy is not definitively known. Many medical professionals believe that there is a link between nausea and the pregnancy hormone known as HCG. Morning sickness and nausea tend to peak at the same time as your HCG levels.

Your nausea will normally begin around 8 weeks, and it can last until your 14th week, or in some cases, even longer. The only true way to combat nausea is by practicing self-care. It is not something that can be avoided or necessarily controlled, but there are ways you can make it easier on yourself. Drinks that include ginger are great for limiting nausea. When you start feeling sick, a glass of ginger ale can do a lot for you. Plain crackers are also very helpful. Keep them close to your bed for times when you feel like you need something in your stomach, yet you cannot keep much down.

Lemons are also great for helping your nausea. Simply smelling a lemon can lessen your chances of vomiting. When all else fails, try to keep your meals as plain as possible. While you might be craving certain flavors, it is better to keep things plain instead of having to vomit later on after eating something with too many ingredients. If certain smells begin to trigger you during your pregnancy, fresh air is very helpful. Step outside when you can, and take some deep breaths to regulate your body.

Listening to your physical symptoms is a smart idea. When you become fatigued, your body is going to be much more prone to vomiting and get sick easily. If you start to feel tired, then give yourself a chance to rest. Just because you used to be able to do certain things before you got pregnant does not mean that you will be able to do all of them during your pregnancy. Your body is going through a lot during this time, so make sure that you are being mindful of this. Even if you do not sleep or nap, lying down can be helpful.

If it ever becomes too much for you to handle, your doctor can prescribe you with anti-nausea pills that will get you through the bad spells that you experience. Some women are just more prone to morning sickness than others. If the at-home remedies do not seem to help you, then you can consult your doctor for something else. Most of the time, these at-home remedies are actually highly effective. Know that it is going to get better, and this nausea isn't going to last forever.

Prenatal Screening and Testing

Throughout your pregnancy, you are going to be guided through many screening and testing sessions to monitor the health of your baby. There are three main prenatal tests that you will go through during each of your trimesters. The purpose of these tests is to identify your baby's blood type, spot any health concerns, and determine the baby's size/gender/position. You are likely most familiar with the test that is done to identify a baby's gender. This is a very commonly awaited test that many parents look forward to. While some prefer to keep the gender a surprise, it has become popular to host a gender reveal party to make a surprise announcement about the gender of your baby. No matter what you choose to do, you can tell the ultrasound technician whether you would like to know the gender or whether you would rather keep it a mystery.

The main difference between screening and diagnostic testing is the depth of the information you can find out. In screenings, you can be presented with the possibility of a problem or health concern. During diagnostic testing, however, you are going to get a more concrete answer. This is going to be a more accurate way for you to find out exactly what is going on with your child in the womb. Your OB-GYN is going to recommend which of these tests and screenings you should have depending on how your pregnancy is going.

Some screenings are recommended for all pregnant women, as they are a routine part of your regular check-ups. You do have the right to refuse a test or a screening if you feel that it isn't going to benefit you. These are all optional, but your OB-GYN should make it clear which tests are routine and beneficial. If you have a certain circumstance surrounding your pregnancy, you might be offered other tests. This usually happens during teen pregnancies, pregnancies with women who are over 35, those with high blood pressure, those with heart or kidney disease, or those prone to asthma.

To decide which tests are right for you, consider the following:

- How accurate is the test?
- What information will it give you?
- Is the procedure painful?
- Will it be dangerous for you or the baby?
- When will you get the results?
- How much does it cost?
- Will your insurance cover it?
- Is there any preparation necessary for the test?

When you gather all of the above information, you will be able to make an educated decision on whether you'd like to go through the process or skip it. This combined with your doctor's advice is how you should be making all medical decisions that pertain to your pregnancy. Since you are going to be offered several tests that you are likely unfamiliar with, it is always best to do your own research before making your final decision.

How to Choose an OB-GYN

There are a few ways that you can go about making your selection, but it is worth asking your current gynecologist if they also practice obstetrics. Since you are already familiar and comfortable with your gynecologist, it makes sense that you might want to use them during your pregnancy, too. If you do not want to use the same doctor, or if you do not have a gynecologist that you visit on a regular basis, there are a few ways to find an OB-GYN. The first is to consult your current healthcare provider. They will normally have a list that you can choose from and they can narrow down the ones that are in your area. This is probably the most helpful way to make your selection.

The reviews matter. You wouldn't want to see an OB-GYN that is known for being rude and untimely, so ensure that you take your time to read the reviews. It is also worth it to ask your friends and family members if they can make any recommendations for you. Hearing real opinions from loved ones that you already trust can become a big influence in your decision-making process. If neither of the above options provides you with any results, you can consult the College of Obstetricians and Gynecologists' website to do a search in your local area.

Only you are going to be able to know who is right for you, but there are some other criteria that you can consider while making your decision. If you have any chronic illnesses or preexisting conditions, you might need to see a specialist who is familiar with these conditions. These OB-GYNs are going to be known for handling high-risk pregnancies. You must also consider each doctor's outlook and methodology that is used in their practice. Each OB-GYN is going to follow a different philosophy and set of techniques, and you need to make sure that these all fall in line with what you want for yourself and your baby.

When you are seeing a new doctor for the first time, think about the appointment as your trial period. See if you feel comfortable in the office and speaking with the doctor and their staff. You must be able to ask questions if necessary, so an office that dismisses your questions is not going to be a great choice for you. During your pregnancy, you are going to be experiencing many things for the first time, so being able to ask all the questions you have is a must. You should never feel like your questions are dumb or excessive. It is your right as the mother to know what is going on with your baby and your body during pregnancy. Make sure that your doctor is going to respect your wishes, even if your opinions do not exactly match theirs.

Common Pregnancy Problems and Solutions

The last thing you want to hear as an expecting mother is that there is a problem. Know that, like everything else in life, pregnancy can be unpredictable. Even if you go through all of the preparation necessary to ensure you have a smooth pregnancy, there is always going to be something that happens that you weren't expecting. Making yourself aware of these common problems is going to help you get through them if they become a part of your pregnancy journey. Knowing that there are solutions for all of these problems should help you to feel at ease.

1. Bleeding Gums: It is likely that you aren't going to expect trouble with your mouth during your pregnancy, but this is something that can happen. The same hormones that can cause your sinuses to act up can also cause your gums to bleed. While this is normal, you can help ease the pain by ensuring you are getting plenty of calcium and cutting out some of the sugar in your diet. If you must go to the dentist, remind them that you are pregnant so they do not perform any procedures that will be harmful to the baby.

2. Vaginal Discharge: Just because your periods have stopped during pregnancy does not mean your vagina is going to stop producing discharge. This discharge is usually white and has a mild smell. While there is nothing you can do to prevent the discharge, you can wear panty liners if it begins to bother you. Consult your doctor if you notice it is a yellow or green color with a strong odor, as this can be a sign of an infection.

3. Leg Cramps: Because of the extra weight you are carrying, it is likely that you will encounter cramped legs. While the feeling is unpleasant, you normally have nothing to worry about. By stretching your legs frequently, you can lessen the risk of cramping. Cold compresses are also very helpful. If your pain lasts for a long period of time accompanied by redness, consult your doctor because this could be due to a blood clot.

4. Hemorrhoids: A lot of expectant mothers are shocked to discover that hemorrhoids can be a normal part of pregnancy. While they are very uncomfortable to deal with, Kegel exercises and over-the-counter medication can soothe the area. Another way to treat existing ones is to try soaking a cotton pad in witch hazel and gently rubbing the area.

5. Itchy and Leaking Nipples: During your pregnancy, your breasts are going through the process of producing milk to feed your baby. While they are growing larger during this process, they can become itchy and potentially start to leak. Using nipple cream can soothe the discomfort. You can also place nursing pads inside your bra to prevent your breast milk from leaking through your shirt.

Working Until You Deliver

You can continue working while you are pregnant until you feel that your symptoms are making it too difficult to complete your normal workday. Legally, an American mother can take up to 12 weeks of maternity leave while having job security. Not all employers pay during this time, so this can vary depending on where you work. Planning on when you are going to take your maternity leave is a very important aspect of your pregnancy. While you might still be able to work a full day, toward the end of your pregnancy you should not be over-exerting yourself. It is better to be cautious than to push yourself and end up getting sick.

If your place of employment does not have an official system for women who need to take maternity leave, you can opt to use the Family and Medical Leave Act. In order to qualify for this, you must work for a covered employer for at least 1 year or longer. You must also work at a location that has 50+ employees within 75 miles.

This is the only law that exists in America to cover you for any type of pregnancy-related leave. Although you will not have to utilize the act as a guarantee, you should still know that it is available for you to use if you meet the qualifications. In an ideal situation, your place of employment will already have a maternity leave system worked out.

At around 15 weeks until your due date, you should give your notice of maternity leave. You can do so by putting it in writing. Much like any major change in your life, you would likely need to inform your boss the same way. Once your notice has been turned in, your boss is going to let you know how much time you are going to be allowed off and if it will or will not be paid. Keeping your rights in mind, know that you can always negotiate at this point. Be reasonable, but also do not settle for something that you find unfair. Having a baby should not be a reason to receive any kind of poor treatment from your superiors at work.

Listen to your body. While there are typical time frames for when expecting mothers usually take maternity leave, you cannot guarantee that your pregnancy is going to allow you the same time frame. You might have different needs or other conditions that cause you to become unable to work a lot sooner than most people. If this applies to your pregnancy, be sure to discuss it with your boss as soon as you can. Remember, there is no reason that you need to overwork yourself during your pregnancy. Not only does it put stress on you, but it puts stress on the baby.

Chapter 5: The First Trimester (1 - 3 Months)

During the first three months of your pregnancy, you are going to experience a lot of new things. Not only are you going to be feeling the symptoms for the first time, but you are also going to be getting into a new routine of regular check-ups and accommodating the changes that your body is experiencing. While it can be easy to feel overwhelmed, having an idea of exactly what is going on during each stage of your pregnancy is going to put you at ease.

The First Month

Your Baby and Your Body

At this stage in your pregnancy, your body isn't likely to go through any visible changes. Since conception has just happened, your baby is a tiny embryo and is still developing. You won't be able to find out any additional details until you are further along, but this does not mean you need to hold back any of your excitement.

The one thing you might notice is that your pregnancy hormones have begun to kick in. This can mean that you will start to experience some pregnancy signs and symptoms that were discussed in the earlier chapter. Whether you have a sudden recognition of particular odors or you feel too emotional for your own good, these are all normal parts of being in your first month of pregnancy.

A slight pressure in your lower abdomen might be noticeable, but it is so slight that it likely won't do anything to change your outward appearance just yet. Some women experience a metallic taste in their mouth during the first month. This is normal, as your taste buds begin to adjust as they will throughout your entire pregnancy. Make sure you are taking your prenatal vitamins so you can keep your vitamin C and Iron levels high enough. Keep your fluid levels high to remain hydrated.

What to Expect at This Check-Up

During your first appointment, you can expect a lot of standard procedures that would happen during normal doctor appointments. You will be weighed, and your blood pressure will be taken. Then, you are going to provide your doctor with a urine sample so they can test your protein and sugar levels. You will also need to provide blood so your doctor can test for anemia and your HCG levels. It is possible that your doctor will also perform a pap smear, a standard procedure that you are likely already used to from your typical visit to the gynecologist. This is going to allow them to spot any abnormalities.

Your Rh can also be tested at this point. This is the protein carried by your red blood cells. You can either be Rh positive (have proteins) or Rh negative (do not have proteins). Why this matters is because your baby is also going to either be Rh positive or negative. If the two of you are not a match, this can become a reason for additional treatment to ensure that your baby is still developing properly.

The first appointment should not include much more than the above. Since it is still too early on to measure your baby and your body, your doctor's main concern is going to be focusing on your physical health and spotting any abnormalities. These appointments typically go by very quickly, and you will not have anything to worry about. The ultrasounds that you are likely looking forward to will not occur until you are around 12 weeks pregnant.

Questions to Ask Your Doctor

Remember, there is no right or wrong way to ask your doctor questions. If you have any questions at all, be vocal about them! It is your doctor's job to inform you of anything you are unsure of. As your body is about to undergo many changes, you will feel better when you can be aware of what exactly is happening and what you are feeling.

You can ask if your doctor has a nurse line that you can call in case you have any questions in the future. This will be helpful if you have a question that cannot wait until your next appointment. Also, ask your doctor what would be considered an emergency. Many expecting mothers do not know what qualifies, and knowing what to look for regarding whether or not to go to the hospital is essential. During this time, you can discuss any changes in your habits or lifestyle that must be made. If you have any questions about the testing, bring them up to your doctor. Ask them which tests they recommend to you at this point in your pregnancy and why.

How to Pamper Yourself During Pregnancy

Staying off your feet is one of the main ways that you can give yourself a break when you are pregnant. Even in your first month of pregnancy, you are naturally going to feel more fatigued than you usually would. Think about the way you feel when you are PMSing. Simple activities such as running errands and even doing simple chores around the house can feel like a big deal. Kicking your feet up for a few moments at a time can help to lessen this exhaustion.

Massages are safe during your first month of pregnancy. Whether you choose to receive one from your significant other or a spa professional, they can help to relax your muscles. As your body begins this significant change, you are going to experience new kinds of aches and pains. Massages help to keep your body loose and relaxed during your pregnancy.

Allow yourself to go shopping for a comfortable pair of pajamas and slippers. Whether you prefer to wear nightgowns or you'd like to opt for a top/bottom set, get a pair that is comfortable. When you can allow yourself to fully relax, your body is going to naturally recharge to the best of its ability.

The Second Month

Your Baby and Your Body

During your 8th week of pregnancy, your baby should be about the size of a raspberry. Compared to only one month ago, this is a huge development from a simple embryo. At this time, your baby's essential organs have begun to develop. With a heart rate of around 150-170 beats per minute, your baby's heart is beating nearly twice as fast as yours. Though you won't be able to feel any of their movements just yet, know that they are becoming more active. Spontaneous twitches start happening in the second month of pregnancy.

Though you might not be showing yet, your clothes are likely going to feel tighter in the second month around the abdomen. This happens because your uterus is also expanding in order to accommodate your baby. It is going to be around the size of a large grapefruit at this point. Morning sickness is likely to become a common occurrence during your second month. It can feel hard to keep anything down at all. Do your best to consume plenty of fruit. Not only is it healthy for you, but it will also provide you with the necessary vitamins and minerals that you need while you are pregnant. If you can't keep anything down, you are going to be losing a lot of these vitamins.

What to Expect at This Check-Up

Your next appointment is likely going to mirror your first. You will go through the same basic procedures such as blood testing and checking your blood pressure. During your first trimester, you are only going to be seeing your OB-GYN once per month, unless you have certain circumstances that would require you to go more frequently. Unfortunately, you still won't be able to see or hear anything at this appointment, but you are getting closer to being able to have an ultrasound.

Until this happens, your doctor's main concern is going to be ensuring that your pregnancy is still following a healthy path. Since this is still early on in the pregnancy, there is a good chance that they would be able to catch any abnormalities if some were to develop. Think about this appointment as yet another chance to become informed. Take notes of your symptoms and discuss them with your doctor if you feel inclined.

Questions to Ask Your Doctor

Aside from any symptoms that you'd like to discuss, you can bring up your preferences for your upcoming ultrasound. A lot of expecting mothers normally have an idea of whether they would like to have a traditional ultrasound or 3D or even 4D ultrasound. As we go more in-depth in later chapters, you will be able to decide if a 4D ultrasound is something that you'd like to do. As much as women do enjoy being able to see their baby at such a high definition and see movements, it requires different equipment.

Most insurance will not cover it, as well. Don't forget, there is also a 3D method that will show your baby in 3D without the movement that the 4D ultrasound offers.

If you have any questions about your baby's rate of development, this is when you should ask your doctor. Finding out that your baby is growing at a normal rate can feel very reassuring, even when you didn't suspect that anything was wrong in the first place. It is nice to hear it directly from your doctor at the moment. Allow the doctor to reassure you about anything that you have been wondering about in the last couple of months.

Weight Gain

In the upcoming months of your pregnancy, people are going to comment on your weight gain. Whether they believe that you have barely gained any weight or if they feel that you are noticeably larger, it has become very common for others to remark about a pregnant woman's weight. This is something that you might not be used to at first, especially if you are particularly sensitive about the topic. Know that most people do not realize that this can come off as rude or an invasion of personal comfort. No matter how much you prepare for your body to undergo this change, the hardest part can be getting used to the comments that you hear from others.

On average, you are only going to gain around 25-35lbs of pregnancy weight. Of course, this can greatly vary due to your natural stature and the size of your baby. Thinking about it in these terms, the number isn't that large at all. The reason why it is more noticeable is that it is almost all going directly to your belly. You should feel proud of this weight that you have gained. It is a sign that you are carrying a healthy baby inside, and if you didn't gain any weight, your baby would not have adequate room to develop.

During your first trimester, you probably aren't going to gain more than 5lbs. This just shows how quickly the rest of the weight is gained. Aside from making room inside your belly for your baby, your body is going to distribute the rest of the weight in a few other places. You'll notice that your breasts are going to get larger, and your overall fluid levels are going to increase. This can add weight to your entire body in a subtle, yet noticeable, way. There are some fluids, and even an organ, that didn't exist before you became pregnant! The placenta develops as your baby grows, and this can account for around 1-2lbs on its own. As you begin gaining more weight, you can think of it as a way that your body is becoming stronger to carry your baby.

The Third Month

Your Baby and Your Body

As you enter your third month of pregnancy, your baby is going to be around the size of a lime. Your baby has already begun producing hormones of their own. Their bone marrow is creating white blood cells so they will be able to defend against any germs or bacteria that are encountered. Your baby can be anywhere from 2 - 2 ¼ inches long at this point. While all of this growth has been occurring on the inside, it shouldn't be surprising if you still aren't really showing on the outside. Don't worry because it is going to happen very soon.

Your uterus has likely begun its migration. Normally situated at the bottom of your pelvis, it will move to the front and center of your abdomen. If you had been experiencing frequent urination in the past months, this symptom should be lessened as your uterus migrates because it is taking some of the pressure off of your bladder. Now that you are approaching your second trimester, your nausea and tender breasts should be easing up as well. In general, many of your early pregnancy symptoms should be alleviated very soon. As nice as this can be, your symptoms can be replaced with a new one - dizzy spells. Feeling lightheaded is a common symptom that tends to appear during the second trimester.

What to Expect at This Check-Up

You will finally get to hear your baby's heartbeat at this check-up! This is the moment you and your significant other has been long awaiting, the one that makes everything feel so much more real. Getting to hear your baby's heartbeat is a special moment that you will never forget. It is likely to be the highlight of your 3rd appointment. Much like the other 2 appointments you have been to, the same testing will be completed to ensure that your baby is still developing as normal.

By request, it is at this appointment that you can ask your doctor for the NTD test. This is the one that can identify Down syndrome in your child. Through blood tests, your doctor will be able to provide you with more information. Since it is an optional test with additional blood work to be done, know that you do not have to opt-in. The decision is purely personal, and it will not impact the development of the Down syndrome gene in your baby either way. It is solely available for informational purposes. Another additional test you can ask your doctor for is Amniocentesis. This is another diagnostic test that can screen for many genetic diseases. Again, this is not mandatory, so do not feel pressured to get it done.

Questions to Ask Your Doctor

As you approach your delivery, it is great to be as prepared as possible. Training your muscles to work with you during this process is going to help the ease of your delivery when the time comes. Ask your doctor about different Kegel exercises you can practice in order to strengthen the core muscles that you will need to use. Kegels can even shorten the amount of time you spend in labor and speed up your post-birth recovery time. Overall, they are great to do at any stage of your pregnancy. Making them a regular part of your routine during your third month will give you plenty of time to perfect them.

Just as you would at any other appointment, you can discuss any symptoms that you have been experiencing lately. If anything has been particularly bothersome to you during the last few months, mention it to your doctor. There might be a medication or technique that will help make things more bearable. Consider mentioning to your doctor if you would like to know the gender of your baby. The timing for this is quickly approaching, so it helps to give your doctor an idea of your preference. It is something that you have probably been thinking about during your entire first trimester, and it is important.

Figuring Out Your Due Date

There are several different methods of figuring out your due date. The following are a few that you can utilize if you'd like to know when you can expect your little bundle of joy to arrive.

While your doctor will be able to provide a more accurate date during your next appointment, these are some things you can do in the meantime to calculate it on your own:

- First Day of Last Period: Since a typical pregnancy lasts for 40 weeks, you can use the first day of your last period as a guide. By adding 40 weeks, or 280 days, to this date, you will be able to figure out an estimate.

- Conception Date: If you know your exact date of conception, a similar method can be applied. Taking this date, simply add 266 days to this date in order to figure out your due date. Many people do not know of their exact conception date, so don't be discouraged if you don't remember yours either.

- Online Calculators: With all of the resources that are available online, there are certainly ways that you can check what your due date will be by using a method like this. Some websites make it super easy to input minimal information that will automatically be calculated for you.

Chapter 6: The Second Trimester

During your second trimester, you will likely notice the most physical changes in your body. From not showing very much to showing a significant amount, you are truly going to be feeling all of the physical aspects of being pregnant. This is normally a time when a pregnancy announcement is made, so you will be able to share this news you have been keeping a secret with your friends and family. It is a very exciting time to experience as a couple and as an expecting mother.

The Fourth Month

Your Baby and Your Body

Though your baby's eyes are still closed, they are developed and able to make small side-to-side movements. The size of an avocado now, your baby's heart can pump around 25 quarts of blood each day. Amazingly, at the 16-week mark, your baby can already develop a thumb-sucking habit. This reflex develops very early on, and it is crazy to think that your little one might already be sucking their thumb from inside the womb.

Your bump is likely going to be pretty apparent at this point. You will notice that some of your clothes don't fit the way they used to. This might call for a maternity shopping spree. Make sure you buy loose-fitting clothing that is comfortable because comfort should be your main priority at this point in your pregnancy. Your breasts are also going to continue growing. They might be feeling especially sore or tender at this point. Remember, they are growing in order to support the milk production that will eventually feed your baby if you choose to breastfeed.

What to Expect at This Check-Up

At this appointment, you will get to listen to your baby's heartbeat again. You will also get to know more about the size and development of your little one. At this point, you will have the option to schedule an ultrasound. This is a very exciting moment in your pregnancy because you will finally get to see your baby. Though your baby will show up on the scan fairly clearly, the external genitalia might not be very visible at this point. Don't worry too much because you should be able to find out about your baby's gender very soon.

If your doctor can't determine the gender at this appointment, they might be able to do so in a few more weeks. It can be hard to stay patient, but if you want accurate information, this patience is a must. Enjoy the moments of being able to see your child and rest assured that your doctor is checking for any and all abnormalities during your pregnancy so far.

Questions to Ask Your Doctor

One of the main questions you will want to ask your doctor about is your baby's gender. Whether you would like to know, would like to keep it a surprise until delivery, or would like to have the results placed in an envelope for a gender reveal party, you should ask your doctor about your options now. You can also ask about your weight gain if you are curious. A lot of women like to know where they fall on the scale in terms of average weight gain for this point of pregnancy.

If you are curious about additional testing, you can ask your doctor if they have any recommendations for you. At this point in your pregnancy, your doctor is going to have a pretty good idea of what you should and should not do. It doesn't hurt to ask for some advice if you are unsure if you should endure any additional testing. Even if you decide to continue on without doing another test, you can at least feel reassured that you asked for your doctor's opinion.

How to Safely Work Out

While you might not be able to work out the way you used to before you got pregnant, exercise is still going to be beneficial for both yourself and the baby. Swimming is a great and safe way to get some exercise without overworking yourself. It allows you to experience a little bit of cardio mixed with a fun way to spend your time. If you decide to exercise in a more traditional way, ensure that you are keeping everything low-impact. You can still lift weights, but make sure they are no more than 5-10lbs. The last thing that you need is to strain your body on top of all the pregnancy symptoms you are experiencing.

No matter what you decide to do, keeping the exercise to around 30 minutes each day is about the average amount you should be getting. Whether you take 3 10-minute walks per day or swim for 30 minutes straight, it is up to you how you'd like to distribute this time.

Gender Reveal

If you decide that you'd like to find out your baby's gender, there are a few ways you can go about doing this. Some couples prefer to find out in private at the doctor's office, and then they will come up with ways to tell their loved ones the great news. In more recent popularity, couples have been holding gender reveal parties. This happens even when the couple does not know the results yet, and then they hold a party where the gender is revealed to all.

A lot of people will give the results to a bakery, and then the bakery will make a cake with either pink or blue inside to signify the gender. Upon cutting into the cake at the party, everyone gets to find out the gender at the same time. No matter what you decide to do, know that your decision is valid. Even if you'd like to keep the gender a surprise until birth, there is nothing wrong with that. Ultimately, the choice is up to the parents.

The Fifth Month

Your Baby and Your Body

This is a big week for development. Your baby should now be able to kick and punch, so this means that you will likely be feeling a lot of this on the inside as your baby goes through phases of being active. The size of a sweet potato now, you should definitely be able to find out the gender if you haven't been able to already. As your baby continues to grow even bigger and stronger, know that there is still plenty of room inside for this process to happen.

At this point, you are over the halfway point in your pregnancy! With only four months left to go, your baby's reproductive organs have formed. If you are carrying a girl, your baby already has a uterus that is fully formed. For a boy, his testicles are going to be developed and soon to descend. You should be showing a considerable amount at this point, and you will truly feel as though you are eating for two.

Remember that heartburn can also follow, so make sure you keep some antacids nearby. Your hair and nails might be experiencing a surge in growth, and you will be delighted to know that they are stronger and healthier than ever. This is one of the many perks that come along with being pregnant.

What to Expect at This Check-Up

As mentioned, if you haven't been able to get sure confirmation of what you are having, then at this appointment, you will likely be able to find out the gender. Otherwise, the appointment is going to follow the same structure as your typical appointments have in the past. This is a point when you can decide on what kind of ultrasound photo you would like. A traditional 2D ultrasound is performed by placing the wand directly over the gel that is placed on your belly. This helps the scanner pick up the image. This is the most traditional type of ultrasound photo that is chosen by parents.

If you would like a 3D or 4D ultrasound, this process is going to be trickier. In order to capture such an image, you will need to keep in mind that these ultrasounds can heat up your tissues. In some cases, this can create pockets of gas or other bodily fluids, which the impacts are still unknown. It is something that is not necessary to expose your baby to, yet it is understandable why parents opt for these stunning, high-quality images of their little ones. Think carefully about your decision and about all the risks involved. Because there isn't as much information available about the impacts of the technology, many parents choose to stick to their 2D ultrasounds.

Questions to Ask Your Doctor

Aside from any normal questions about your current symptoms, you can ask your doctor their opinion on the various ultrasound options that you have available. While taking a more cutting-edge approach isn't necessary, some parents truly do value having the image that it can capture. Your doctor is going to be able to put your worries at ease and guide you toward the best decision for your personal beliefs.

Remember, you can always change your mind. If you opt for a 2D ultrasound at first, you can consider if you'd like to have a 3D or 4D in the future. Keep this idea in mind when you undergo your first scan. Your doctor should always be there to answer all of your questions about the different processes and the pros and cons of each one.

Now would also be the time to bring up any questions you may have regarding your diet. If you have noticed a spike in your hunger, you are probably eating more than you were in the past. Consult your doctor on whether you are getting enough vitamins and nutrients in your current diet. They will be able to tell you if you need to make any adjustments or if you need any supplements.

Sex during Pregnancy

This far along in your pregnancy, you are probably wondering if sex is going to be safe for the baby. It is no secret that your pregnancy hormones are going to have you feeling frisky toward your partner. Some expecting mothers have stated that their hormones had them feeling more turned on than ever. This can be very overwhelming, especially when you are worried about doing anything that will be damaging to the baby. To put any myths to rest, having sex with penetration is not going to harm or damage your baby.

The only thing to worry about during sex while pregnant is finding a position that is comfortable for you. You might have to try out several new positions with your partner that allow you to take the pressure off of your stomach. Consider lying on your side with your partner behind you. This tends to be a fairly comfortable position for women at this stage of pregnancy. If you can't find any positions that allow you to stay comfortable during penetrative sex, know that oral sex is also going to feel great at this point in your pregnancy. This can allow you to lie on your back with the help of some pillows to prop you up.

The Sixth Month

Your Baby and Your Body

You are nearly there! Now as big as a pomegranate, your baby should be putting on a lot more weight. Aside from accumulating more fat, your baby is also going to be gaining muscle mass. Any hair, from the head to the eyelashes, should still be white and transparent. Since their auditory system is forming rapidly, you might notice that your baby will have a music preference and will enjoy hearing the sound of your voice. You can tell by the way that they respond in the womb. Now at around 11-inches long, your baby likely weighs 1lb.

The biggest change you'll probably notice, other than your ever-growing belly, is the shape of your belly button. If you formerly had an innie, it should now resemble an outie. This is going to return to normal after you give birth. Some new symptoms you might become familiar with are swollen wrists and fingers. This can cause a feeling of numbness, and it can get in the way of your daily routine as well as your work, depending on what you do for a living. Your palms might even begin to itch. Expect to feel an increase in headaches and blurry vision, as well. These are all normal symptoms to experience in your sixth month.

What to Expect at This Check-Up

During this check-up, your doctor is likely to go over your birth plan. Even if you don't know exactly what you'd like that to be just yet, you will be encouraged to decide as the time is quickly approaching. Many expecting mothers do not know what they would like their birth plan to be at this point, but it is smart to begin thinking about it sooner rather than later. Consider where you would feel most comfortable with giving birth and what method you would like to aim for. Know that, even with a detailed birth plan, your birth can happen in an entirely different way depending on the circumstances involved with your labor. You can ask your doctor about what all of the different options are.

Aside from the normal testing that you will go through, your doctor will likely want to run a glucose test on you at this point. This involves drinking a special liquid that will allow doctors to see clearer results. They will likely give you the drink to take home, and then you will be instructed when to drink it and when to come back to get your blood drawn. Other than this, there should not be anything new or unfamiliar during your check-up.

Questions to Ask Your Doctor

The main questions you should be asking your doctor at this appointment should revolve around your birth plan. Whether you have done extensive research on your own or no research yet, your doctor is going to be able to inform you about all of the different ways that a woman can choose to give birth. Keep in mind that not everyone decides to give birth in a hospital. Some women prefer to be in the comfort of their own homes. While this can present risks, as long as you are having a typical course of pregnancy, there is no reason why you shouldn't be able to have a home birth as well. Your doctor will be able to confirm or deny this for you.

There is also the option to have your baby in a birthing center rather than a hospital. This involves guidance from a doula or midwife in a setting that is less clinical than a traditional medical facility. Your doctor will likely be able to tell you about the risks of this as well as recommend a center that is close to your area.

Another thing to consider is whether or not you'd like the epidural. While there are risks and complications involved, many mothers still opt for the epidural because the pain becomes too unbearable. You aren't necessarily going to be able to predict your level of pain tolerance until you are giving birth, but your doctor can explain the process of getting the epidural and what it involves.

Childbirth Education

Consider taking some childbirth classes with your partner at this point in your pregnancy. These classes are meant to teach you about everything you need to know before, during, and after your delivery. For first-time parents, it can be helpful to walk through each step that is going to happen when the time comes. Not only will you be more informed on *how* to deliver your baby, but you are also going to feel more confident in your ability to do so.

Your instructor will be able to go over various breathing and relaxation techniques with you that can either be performed solo or with the help of your partner. They will show you how you can get through the delivery while relying on the support and help of your partner, too. Some classes even include a tour of the birthing facility of your choosing. Becoming familiar with it beforehand can do a lot to put you at ease when you go into labor. These classes create a special bond between you and your significant other. They will show you how to prepare for the miraculous experience to come.

Chapter 7: The Third Trimester

You have finally made it into the last trimester! This is the final stretch, and before you know it, you will be holding your baby in your arms. As you approach your due date, you should be feeling confident and prepared. You have likely already begun to arrange the nursery in your home that your baby will soon inhabit. These are the last few things you must know before you deliver your newborn.

The Seventh Month

Your Baby and Your Body

Now as big as a head of lettuce, your baby can experience the REM cycle. This series of rapid eye movements indicate that your baby is able to fall into a deep pattern of sleep. There is also a high likelihood that your baby can dream! At this point, your baby will be able to open and close their eyes and blink too. A baby in the womb at this point can also make faces and stick out their tongue. Doctors don't know exactly why they do this, but some believe it is because the baby is tasting the amniotic fluid.

Since your baby is getting settled into the proper position to be delivered, you are likely going to be feeling a lot of pressure in your lower region. You are likely to feel more uncomfortable at this point in your pregnancy because of this new pressure and your baby's ability to move freely, kicking and squirming often. Your feet might be swollen more, and you might notice that your back is continuously aching. Make sure that you are paying attention to your body and staying off your feet as much as possible. Since your uterus is much enlarged at this point, it is possible you will feel shooting pains down your spine known as sciatica. This is nerve pain that happens due to the pressure being put on the lower nerve in your spine.

What to Expect at This Check-Up

In your third trimester, you are going to possibly be introduced to a new test. An NST, or non-stress test, is actually not stressful at all. It is done to examine your baby's heart rate and movement. Not all women receive this test, but if you do, this does not necessarily indicate that anything is wrong. Some women with smaller babies receive it by default. It only takes around 20-40 minutes to perform. A belt monitor will be placed around your belly, and during this time, you will be given a button to press each time you feel your baby move. This gives your doctor an idea of how active your baby is and how reactive they are.

Your doctor will also likely do a vaginal exam, which includes feeling the position of your baby. It is important to know how your baby is sitting at this point because this is going to be an indication of whether you can have a natural birth or whether you might be forced to have a C-section. While it is still early to claim either of these things for sure, your doctor will have some kind of idea of how your baby is going to continue to drop and which way they will be facing.

Questions to Ask Your Doctor

This appointment will be a great time to ask about where your baby is currently located and what position they are in. You can ask if this is an ideal position, or if your doctor thinks that the baby is going to be moving in a way that is going to make the delivery a little bit more complicated. Of course, your doctor won't always be able to predict exactly what position your baby will be in as you go into labor, but the patterns that are currently forming will provide them with a good indication of what to expect.

Keep in mind that you might have to deviate from your original birth plan, as mentioned before. Talk to your doctor about the process of changing the birth plan mid-delivery. When you can feel prepared for this, it becomes less scary to think about the possibility. Your doctor and the entire staff present during your delivery are going to know what the safest option is for your baby and yourself at the moment. Having this trust in them comes from being able to ask all of your questions and express any concerns that you might have. If you are still uncertain about some aspects of your birth plan, this would be an excellent time to lock them in with your doctor.

How to Sleep

Getting enough sleep when you are uncomfortable can be difficult. As a pregnant woman, you are going to learn about several different things that can assist you with staying comfortable and getting enough rest. When you wake up cranky and exhausted, your pregnancy symptoms can feel amplified. A lot of women experience insomnia during pregnancy, and some even experience RLS (Restless Leg Syndrome). These two factors alone can completely destroy your sleep schedule.

While there is no magic pill that can fix these things, you can make sure that you are sticking to bedtime that is reasonable. If you plan what time you'd like to sleep and when you'd like to wake up, this allows you to have somewhat of a sleep schedule. You can also try sleeping on your left side. This is known to allow the most relief for a pregnant woman, and it can feel incredibly comfortable compared to most other sleep positions.

Make sure that you are drinking enough fluids throughout the day. Being dehydrated is only going to promote exhaustion. Drinking more is going to mean peeing more, but this is healthy for you. Put a night light in your bathroom to avoid having to turn on the light and completely wake yourself up. The night light will be less harsh on your eyes.

Easing Labor Pain

As you approach your delivery date, you are likely going to be anticipating the contractions and pain that you will endure. While it can vary based on your pregnancy and individual pain tolerance, the following are some tips to get you through it:

- Rhythmic Breathing: The way that you breathe is going to be your main form of control during contractions. Breathing techniques that you learn during classes, or on your own, will help to soothe the pain. By focusing on your breathing, you will be able to release tension. Taking a quick breath every 2-3 seconds can help to alleviate what you are feeling.

- Heat: A hot water bottle can feel nice on your lower back when you are experiencing labor pains. This heat is going to loosen your muscles, further prepping your body for the delivery. Because of all the tension, your pain sensors are going to be heightened. Allow yourself to relax into the heat.

- Movement: Sometimes, getting up and walking can help take your mind off the pain. When you are in labor, you do not necessarily need to be bedridden. The staff at the hospital will likely encourage you to get up and walk around your room if you want to!

- Gentle Massage: A gentle hand massage or back massage can do a lot to ease your nerves. Having your partner or doula massage you every so often will keep you in the relaxed state of mind for an easy birth.

The Eighth Month

Your Baby and Your Body

Right now, all of your baby's organs are fully formed except for their lungs. Your baby is still going to be inhaling amniotic fluid for practice using their lungs. Their skin is now opaque, and they are about as big as a cantaloupe! At around 4lbs and 16 inches, delivery is going to happen very soon.

Because your body is so close to having to deliver, you might start to experience what are known as Braxton Hicks contractions. This occurs when you notice your uterus tightening or hardening every so often. A lot of women mistake these contractions for labor contractions. Think about them as a rehearsal for what your body is about to do.

At nighttime, you are probably experiencing more leg cramping and tightness. The feeling of dizziness is also likely going to increase. As your breasts continue to grow in size, you might experience some leakage. This is normal, and the fluid leaking out is known as colostrum, which is what your breasts produce before breast milk.

What to Expect at This Check-Up

This visit should be routine for the most part. The same normal procedures will take place in order to monitor your health and the health of your baby. Your doctor might have you do a vaginal/rectal culture which is used for the purpose of testing for Group B Strep. This can be harmful to your baby if it is present during the time of your delivery, so your doctor will likely check for it sometime around this appointment, if not the next one.

Questions to Ask Your Doctor

Now is the time to go over any additional details of your birth plan that you wish to discuss with your doctor. You don't have much time until your due date, so many unanswered questions should be taken care of at this appointment. A lot of women deliver early, so it is a good idea to have all of this information locked down well ahead of time. As usual, you can also discuss any symptoms that you have been having recently with your doctor. The discomfort is likely going to be increasing due to your size, and your doctor might have some advice on how you can stay comfortable.

Breastfeeding

Breastfeeding is a highly beneficial choice to make for your baby. Since your body is naturally producing this milk, it makes sense that it will have all of the nutrients that your newborn needs. If you are undecided on whether you would like to breastfeed, consider the following benefits that come with it:

- Protection Against Allergies and Eczema: Certain proteins in cow's milk and soy milk formula can stimulate an allergic reaction in your newborn. These proteins can be harder for your baby to digest, therefore creating a higher likelihood of certain allergies and even eczema.

- Less Stomach Upset: As mentioned, your breast milk is going to contain everything that your baby needs in terms of nutrients, so naturally, they are going to be able to easily digest it. A newborn's stomach is very sensitive, so this can help them transition into drinking cow's milk or formula in the future.

- Reduces Risk of Viruses: Through infant nutrition research, it has been shown that breastfed babies are less likely to get sick during their infant months. The statistics actually show that babies who are not breastfed are three times more likely to get ear infections than those who breastfeed. They can even be five times more likely to get pneumonia (Lucla, C. A., Hartshorn, J., n. d.).

- Makes Vaccines More Effective: As your baby grows up, they are going to be receiving vaccinations of your choosing. A breastfed baby is known to have antibodies that are more responsive to these vaccines as opposed to a baby who was never breastfed.

- Lose Pregnancy Weight: Your baby is not the only one who will benefit from breastfeeding. While it is a wonderful bonding experience for a mother to have with her child, it can also be a way for you to begin your weight loss after pregnancy. Producing breast milk actually burns around 300-500 calories each day!

The Ninth Month

Your Baby and Your Body

At this point in the pregnancy, your baby has done most of the in-womb growing already. The growth is going to slow down, and you will feel your baby dropping lower in order to get into a proper delivery position. As big as a bundle of kale now, your baby's hearing is going to be extra sharp during this final month of pregnancy.

You will notice that your walk has changed quite a bit during this final stretch of pregnancy. This occurs because your hips are widening and your baby is dropping. This is a natural occurrence and it is your body's way of showing you that it is ready to deliver the baby. During this time, it is normal to experience pain in your pelvic region. Expect a lot of bloating, cramping, and even passing of gas or burping.

What to Expect at This Check-Up

During this appointment, you are likely going to receive your pre-registration paperwork from your doctor to the hospital or birthing center of your choice. Your weight and blood pressure will be checked, as it normally is, and the baby's statistics will also be checked. You will be asked for a urine sample in order to check your sugar and protein levels. Your doctor will also likely ask you about your baby's movements since last time. Then, the height of your uterus will be measured in order to track just how much the baby has grown.

At this point, your doctor will likely inform you about all of the signs you need to be aware of to determine if you are going into labor. Keeping in mind that you might give birth before your due date, it is important that you know what to look for. Your urinary habits might also be discussed. It is common for women to leak slightly when they cough or laugh because of all the pressure being put on the bladder.

Questions to Ask Your Doctor

You can ask your doctor about your mobility from this point onward. A lot of women are advised not to travel too far from home or the hospital in case they were to go into labor. You can also ask about what you should do if you believe that you are going into preterm labor. At this stage in the pregnancy, a lot can happen very quickly, so you will want to make sure that you are prepared to give birth at any moment. Your doctor can go over the process with you for what happens after your water breaks and you realize that you are ready to give birth. No matter where you are or what you are doing, this can be an exhilarating experience. You are about to meet your little one, yet you want to do it safely. Make sure you have a clear understanding of what you need to do when you see the signs.

Pre-Labor, False Labor, and Real Labor

Pre-Labor: Before you are about to go into labor, you will begin having contractions. This is your body's way of warning you that it is almost time to give birth. Before you actually go into labor, the contractions will be short and irregular. A day or so before you give birth you might notice a discharge that appears bloody. This is likely your mucus plug, and it is normal to lose this around this time in the pregnancy. It is not always noticed, but if you do see something like this, it should be a pinkish color that is the texture of mucus.

False Labor: While contractions are a big indication that you are going into labor, their frequency will ultimately be able to tell you if you are in real labor or false labor. In the latter, the contractions are going to be irregular and without progression. They will feel like a general period cramp.

Real Labor: When your water breaks, this is a big sign that labor has begun. Do not panic if yours does not break on its own because some women need assistance at the hospital to have theirs broken. Your contractions will now feel strong, starting from your lower back and extending down to your abdomen and groin. They will be progressively longer and stronger. Signs of active labor will mean that you are having contractions that last for around 45-60 seconds and are 3-4 minutes apart. When you notice this kind of regularity and frequency, then it is time for you to get to the hospital and get ready for delivery. Some women only stay in labor for a few hours, while others can stay in labor for a few days. Each pregnancy is going to be different, but your doctor is going to be there to guide you through the process.

Chapter 8: Labor and Delivery

The moment has finally arrived, and it is time to deliver your baby! This process is normally a mixture of a whirlwind and a waiting game. While you are going to be very excited to meet your new baby, there are a few steps that you must go through in order to have a safe and successful delivery. From knowing what to bring with you to the hospital to figuring out how to manage your pain, this chapter is going to teach you everything you need to know in order to give birth.

How to Pack

While there are some essentials that you will need with you at the hospital, you also need to make sure that you are going to be comfortable. Likely, you will be in the hospital for a couple of days, so make sure that you pack enough to last you for your entire stay. If you need help deciding what to bring, this sample list can help you make sure that you aren't forgetting anything:

- Your birth plan/maternity notes
- Something comfortable to wear during labor
- Something to wear home from the hospital
- A few changes of clothes
- A robe
- Slippers
- Socks
- Snacks and drinks
- Entertainment (books, magazines, phone, tablet, laptop)
- Lip balm
- Your favorite pillow
- Hair ties
- Massage oil or lotion
- Toiletries

What you pack is mainly going to keep you busy. Since you might be in labor for a long time before you actually begin pushing or delivering your child, having several different ways to pass the time is going to help you. Make sure that you do not run out of things to do that you can easily accomplish from your hospital bed. If you do decide you'd like to get up and walk around, hospitals can be chilly. This is why bringing a robe/socks/slippers is important.

Ideally, you will want to pack all of this stuff several days before you anticipate going into labor. It is never a good idea to leave the packing until the last minute. The bag should be packed and waiting in your closet until the time comes. With everything that you need inside, you can simply have your partner grab the bag so you can be out the door quickly. Plus, when you pack ahead of time, you can ensure that you aren't forgetting anything.

Remember that your partner should also pack a bag. While you are the only one going into labor, your partner is likely going to be in the hospital for the same amount of time. While they will have the ability to leave if necessary, it is still better to ensure that they pack for a few days as well. Many couples prepare the mother, and when the time comes, the significant other is left scrambling to stuff clothing into a bag. Keep both bags packed well ahead of time and you will both be prepared.

Labor and Numbness

While you are probably already familiar with the epidural, you should also know about a pudendal block. This is something that is given as a shot vaginally before delivery. It will numb your vaginal area entirely but know that it is not going to stop the pain from contractions like the epidural will. This is a quick-acting fix and it will make your vagina feel numb. For some women, this is a happy medium between no pain relief and an epidural. The choice is up to you, but it is always good to know all of your options ahead of time.

If you are thinking about having something that is more cohesive to the pain that you will be experiencing, you might want to consider a spinal or epidural. Both of these options are used in order to numb certain parts of your body to assist you with pain relief. The spinal is a single shot of medicine that is best for short-term delivery situations. This type of pain relief is usually given to women who are having C-sections. The epidural stays in your back through a catheter. This allows the doctor to provide you with more medicine if necessary. When the doctor does not know how long the labor is going to last, this is likely the option that is going to be offered.

Whether you choose one of the above options or none, this does not make you a bad mother or an unfit mother. We all experience pain differently, and this process should be as calm for you as possible. When you are calm, the baby stays calm. A mother who is in distress can end up with a baby who is in distress. As you think about the options that are available, know that you might also change your mind during active labor. While having a plan is great and recommended, feeling your labor pains at the moment will tell you what is going to work best for you.

Epidural or Epidural-Free?

The decision to get an epidural is one that you are going to encounter as you enter active labor. Plenty of women opt for the epidural in order to better manage their pain, yet a lot of mothers do not wish to utilize any kind of pain drug during labor because they feel it is better for the baby. There can often be a stigma surrounding whether or not you get the epidural, but at the end of the day, this is your decision to make. As mentioned, everyone has a different pain tolerance and belief about the safety of the epidural.

Having a natural birth does not make you a better or more capable mother. If you decide you need the epidural, then you need to do what is best for you and what is best for the baby. Remember that the more stress you experience, the more stress the baby is going to feel. This can impact your ease of delivery when it comes time to push. These are a few things that you must keep in mind when you are making your decision.

To make a more educated decision, it helps to know the pros and cons of getting an epidural:

Pros

- Painless delivery
- Better for prolonged labor
- Potentially lowered blood pressure
- Can speed up delivery
- Useful in case of a C-section because the mother is still alert

Cons

- Back pain/soreness
- Persistent bleeding at the puncture site
- Fever
- Difficulty breathing

- Potential dangerous drop in blood pressure

Much like your birth plan, you are going to probably have your choice in mind before you go into labor. Know that this plan can change at any point in time once you are getting ready to deliver your baby, and that is okay. The risks associated with getting the epidural, come from the idea that, since the mother can't feel everything that is going on, this can lead to complications. While this isn't always the case, it is something to keep in mind. Another reason why mothers choose to deliver naturally is that they do not want their newborn being exposed to any medication that comes through getting the epidural. There is no right or wrong decision, though; you need to do what feels best.

Beyond Pain Relief

Going into your delivery while being fearful of the pain is only going to stress you out. No matter what medication you decide to take or to pass on, the most important thing for you to do is to remain calm. This is something that you should be practicing in the months leading up to your delivery. Working on communicating with your partner is going to help you when the moment finally arrives.

As long as you can remember to breathe and feel that you can rely on your partner for support, you are going to be just fine while you deliver your baby. Having distractions can be a great way to pass the time when you first enter labor. The process can take a long time, and having someone to talk to is going to help you get through it. Talking to your partner or a loved one is a way to remain calm while also focusing on something else at the moment.

As your contractions come and go you need to keep your body as loose as possible. If you tense up each time, your body is only going to feel more stressed as they get more intense. Remember that this is a happy and amazing time; it will all be worth it once you can hold your baby in your arms for the first time. There is already going to be a lot of adrenaline pumping through your system, and this can act as a medication in itself. Your body knows what to do, so you just need to make sure that you are allowing it to happen in the calmest way you can.

Cesarean Delivery (Pros and Cons)

Pros

- The birth will be more predictable
- It gives mothers who cannot give birth vaginally another option
- The C-section can be scheduled
- Labor will likely be much shorter

Cons

- A longer hospital stay after giving birth
- Increased risk of blood loss
- Longer recovery period
- A scar on the lower abdomen

- Baby is at higher risk of developing breathing problems

With a C-section, sometimes it is necessary to have one due to the position of your baby. Other times, women request them. No matter the case, the process is generally fairly simple. The mother will get an IV for fluids. A catheter is placed inside the bladder to remove any urine. The doctor will make a single horizontal incision in the lower abdomen, and this will normally serve the dual purpose of rupturing the amniotic sac. Once this has been ruptured, the baby will be removed by the doctor from the uterus.

Sometimes, the doctor can simply pull the baby out by hand, but other times, tools like forceps are necessary. The surgery can take anywhere from 1-2 hours, and the mother remains awake for it. A surgical tarp is normally put up so the woman cannot see what is going on below her torso in order to keep her calm. Some hospitals offer the chance to watch the procedure from a monitor if the mother chooses to see exactly what is happening. Once the baby is out, there is the same option to cut the umbilical cord yourself.

Recovery can take around 6 weeks, with 2-4 additional days spent in the hospital as compared to those who deliver vaginally. Even if you do plan to have a vaginal delivery, if your labor is too prolonged, your doctor is likely going to recommend that you get a C-section for the health of your baby and yourself. It is a faster way to get the baby out, and the doctor can perform any necessary check-ups to ensure that your baby is healthy and that everything is functional.

Home Birth (Pros and Cons)

Giving birth in the comfort of your own home might sound like an amazing alternative to sitting in the hospital for a few days. It is a less clinical setting that a lot of mothers prefer. Naturally, there are going to be risks involved because there will not be a staff of trained medical professionals in your home to assist you if you are having any difficulties, are in need of an emergency C-section, or if the baby is born with complications.

Typically a midwife or doula is going to be present, so you do not have to go through the entire process alone, but keep in mind that they are mainly going to be there for your own moral support. You will not have the option to get an epidural that they would offer in a hospital. Those who know ahead of time that they do not wish to use pain medication have no problem with choosing home birth. There is something incredibly special about giving birthright from the comfort of your own home, and that is something that a lot of people desire. Naturally, you might be scared to go with this option during your first pregnancy since you do not know what to expect.

Talk to your doctor about this option. They are going to be able to give you a realistic answer as to whether or not it is a good idea for you and your baby. Some pregnancies are naturally going to be higher risk than others, and for those, home birth is likely not going to be the best option.

Water Birth (Pros and Cons)

Waterbirth is exactly as it sounds, and it can actually happen from home or in a participating hospital. When you go into labor, you would enter a small, shallow pool of water and give birth to your baby inside of it. If you plan on doing this from home, you can do it in your bathtub, but getting a proper birthing pool is recommended. It will allow you more room to move around, and you will likely feel more comfortable. A lot of women find the idea of wading in a pool of water to be comforting, and it can provide an alternative birthing position from the typical one that is encouraged in the hospital. Giving birth on your back might not be right for you, so water birth allows you to either sit, stand and hang over the edge of the pool, or squat.

Water immersion can be known to shorten the time spent in labor. For most women, the delivery isn't even the hardest part, it is the labor. A lot of women report that giving birth in water is a lot less stressful, which you know is a lot better for the baby. The experience that you have is also more organic and a lot different than the one you would have if you were in a hospital room. A lot of women who opt for a water birth that can have their baby directly into their arms.

Naturally, the complications must be assessed. If you are giving birth in water from home, the same risks are going to apply with not having medical staff on hand to assist you if any complications occur. Also, if the water is too hot, this can begin to overheat and cause fever during delivery. Once the baby is born, it is important to regulate their temperature right away and clear their lungs, nose, and mouth of fluids. You need to make sure that you are ready to do this as soon as the baby is born.

The Aftermath

One of the main worries after giving birth is how long the healing process takes. Women are very resilient. Whether you have an unmedicated vaginal birth, a C-section, or a water birth from home, you are going to need a lot of time to rest. Take bed rest, and enjoy this bonding time with your new baby. There isn't much that you need to know about what happens after you give birth because this is simply when your recovery process begins. As your body heals, you are going to be spending the rest of your time getting to know your baby and creating that irreplaceable bond.

A lot of women wonder when it is safe to begin having sex again after they give birth. While there is no concrete timeline, doctors do say that the highest chance for experiencing risks and infections come within the first 2 weeks after giving birth. As long as you feel up to it and physically ready, then you can start having sex as soon as you want to. Know that, depending on what kind of delivery you had, there will be different levels of pain that likely did not exist before. If it is too painful, try to wait at least a few more days or weeks before you try again. Keep the communication open with your partner on whether you even feel like having sex yet. Your body will have just gone through a lot of intense pain and hard work, so it is perfectly understandable if you are not in the mood right away again. If you are worried about the tightness of your pelvic floor, don't forget to still do your Kegel exercises to ensure that they remain toned.

Chapter 9: You're Having Twins

Finding out that you are pregnant can be life-altering, but finding out that you are pregnant with twins can change even more aspects of your life. It can be fairly easy to prepare for one baby but knowing that you are expecting two might send you into a panic. While there is no need to panic, you probably have a lot of questions about how you need to prepare for the delivery of two healthy babies. The great thing is you are receiving two blessings instead of one, like most women. Having twins can be the most exciting news to receive, and as long as you are prepared, your pregnancy should not be much different than any other traditional pregnancy.

The following are some facts about twin pregnancies that you have likely never heard before:

1. You Are More Likely to Have Twins in

Your 30s or 40s: In a lot of cases, having twins naturally tends to happen to mothers who are already out of their 20s. According to research, after you get out of your 20s, your ovulatory cycles are going to be different. Because of this irregularity, when you do ovulate, you might be ovulating two follicles at once. This is how twin pregnancies happen!

2. You Will Need to Have More Doctor Appointments: When you are pregnant, routine doctor visits are going to become a part of your monthly routine. These appointments happen because your doctor needs to monitor the growth and development of your baby. Naturally, if you are expecting two babies, there will need to be extra monitoring. Two babies are going to be sharing the space that is normally only used by one baby. You can expect to have more ultrasounds if you are expecting twins.

3. Morning Sickness Tends to Be Worse:

Every expectant mother struggles with morning sickness, but those expecting twins will likely see more of this. It is the sudden increase of hormones that typically makes you feel nauseated, so you are going to be getting a double dose of hormones when there are twins involved. The good news is that even despite carrying two babies, the morning sickness tends to fade away between weeks 12-14, just like any other pregnancy.

4. You Won't Feel the Kicking Earlier: It is a common misconception that you will feel your babies moving around sooner than you would if you were having a single baby. Developmentally, your babies are going to be growing at the same rate as any other baby in the womb, so you shouldn't be able to feel any additional movement or kicking any earlier. Fetal movement can tend to feel like gas, so a lot of women might not even realize that the baby/babies are kicking right away.

5. Weight Gain Is Increased: This one seems fairly obvious, but if you are carrying two babies, you are going to probably gain more weight. If you are of average weight for your height and you get pregnant with twins, you can expect to gain around 37-54lbs. A healthy amount of weight gain for a mother carrying twins is no less than 15lbs and no more than 40lbs. Your doctor is going to be monitoring this closely.

6. You Are More Likely to Develop Gestational Diabetes: If you were to develop gestational diabetes when pregnant with twins, one of the main risks is that you will have larger babies and then you will have to deliver by C-section. Gestational diabetes is common during pregnancy at times, but if you develop it while you are pregnant with twins, you will have a higher risk of developing type 2 diabetes later on in life.

7. Labor and Delivery Usually Come Early:

Statistically, mothers who are carrying twins tend to go into labor at around the 36-37 week mark. Because the babies are probably going to be born early, they have more of a risk of developing respiratory issues. The babies might also be born underweight.

What You Need to Know

Knowledge is everything when it comes to pregnancy, and this is especially true when you find out that you are expecting more than one baby. As soon as you get the wonderful news, you can begin planning for the future. Not only do you need to think about your birth plan, but you will also need to consider if your current home is big enough and if you and your partner are financially stable to support these babies. It is never too early to get prepared for your twins. While your body might not feel or look extremely different with twins inside, you have less than a year to prepare to take care of two little bundles of joy.

Make sure that you are keeping your body as strong as possible. Every pregnant woman should be taking prenatal vitamins, but you truly need to make sure that you are getting enough nutrients because two babies are going to be relying on you for nutrition. The exhaustion can feel overwhelming at times, and you are probably going to need to get off your feet a lot to give yourself some much-needed breaks. Keep in mind that you are going to be eating a lot more than you are used to eating. With two babies needing nourishment, you might feel like your stomach is now a bottomless pit.

Folic acid is especially important for twins because they ward off birth defects. The recommended amount is 1mg per day for twin pregnancies, as opposed to 0.4mg for single-baby pregnancies. One of the main birth defects that are seen in twin pregnancies is spina bifida. This is a defect that occurs when the spine is not able to develop correctly, causing complications later on in life. The folic acid is going to keep the babies strong and healthy, ensuring that they can each fully develop.

Spotting is something that can worry any pregnant woman, and that is understandable. When you become pregnant, your period stops as your baby grows inside of your womb. It can be normal to see some spots in a traditional pregnancy, but you might see even more of this if you are having twins. Of course, a mother's first thought when she sees spotting is that she is having a miscarriage. Unfortunately, this can be the case, and it is more common for mothers expecting twins or triplets. If you do notice spotting, you don't need to panic, though.

Light spotting instead of cramps is your body's way of transitioning out of having periods and into being pregnant. If you begin to cramp regularly, pass large blood clots, and remain actively bleeding, then this is going to be more of a cause for concern. If you are ever unsure about the way your body is functioning during your pregnancy, you can always consult your doctor.

It never hurts to ask, and you should definitely feel at ease during your pregnancy because you need to understand what is going on with your body.

It is not impossible to vaginally deliver twins, even triplets, but know that you are likely going to need a C-section when it comes time to deliver your babies. As explained, you are likely going to deliver your babies earlier than a mother who is having a traditional pregnancy. For this reason, your birth plan must be made sooner and your hospital bag should be packed earlier. Everything that you would do for a traditional pregnancy, you need to do just a little bit sooner. Remember, you are going to need to set up two cribs and potentially even two nurseries depending on if you'd like to keep the babies together or in their own rooms. Make sure that you give yourself and your partner enough time to do all of this because the weeks can go by very quickly.

Announcing to your loved ones that you are expecting two bundles of joy can be very fun. Everyone is going to be incredibly excited, and you will probably find that a lot of your friends and family members are going to probably step up to ask if you need any help. Take this help when you can! You will be thankful that you did. Before babies are born, you might not think that you need a lot of help. Things can progress very quickly when you have two crying babies in each arm who need to be fed, though. Be grateful for any help that is offered to you, and know that just because you are capable of doing it only with your partner does not mean that you should have to.

It can seem like your body is going through a lot more than a typical expecting mother's body, but just remember, the duration is not going to be any longer. At most, you will still only need to get through nine months (or less) of pregnancy. Your body is strong and resilient, and it will still know what to do, no matter how many babies you are having at once. A lot of mothers wonder if there are any early signs that can indicate that twins are developing. While there aren't any concrete signs that will surely confirm that you are, here are some symptoms that you can look out for:

- Family History: If someone else in your family has given birth to twins, this automatically increases your likelihood. While chance still is the biggest factor when it comes to how many babies you will have, the twin gene is one that can be passed down from generation to generation.
- Fertility Treatments: If you are having trouble conceiving, you might seek treatments that will increase your chances of becoming pregnant. These hormonal treatments can often work so well that they can potentially give you twins. A lot of women who go through IVF (in vitro fertilization) have been known to become pregnant with twins.

- Higher BMI: Your BMI stands for body mass index. There are plenty of charts that can allow you to track your BMI, or your doctor can let you know what yours is. If you have a higher BMI, this can be a factor in becoming pregnant with twins. Those who have a BMI of 25+ typically have an increased possibility.

Multiple Childbirth

When the time comes to give birth, you might be wondering how it is even possible to deliver more than one baby at a time. To put yourself at ease, know that millions, even billions, of women have gone through this before and have ended up with healthy babies. There is no doubt that your delivery is going to be eventful, but this is normally the most exciting part of the process of birthing twins. There are three main classifications that you need to know about that will determine how you will give birth to the babies:

- Monochorionic monoamniotic (Mo-Mo): This is when your babies are sharing the placenta and amniotic sac.
- Monochorionic diamniotic (Mo-Di): This is when they are sharing a placenta, but they each have their own amniotic sac.
- Dichorionic diamniotic (Di-Di): This is when each of your babies has their own placenta and amniotic sac.

Early into your pregnancy, your doctor will be able to tell you which of the above situations applies. With Mo-Mo twins, concerns normally arise during the delivery time because there is the possibility that the babies could get tangled up in one another's umbilical cords. While this does not always happen, it is standard that Mo-Mo babies are delivered by C-section to prevent this complication altogether. Because this is the safest way to deliver these twins, your doctor is likely going to explain this to you after the first couple of ultrasounds.

Regardless of your babies' classification, your delivery room is still going to be prepared to help you deliver either vaginally or by C-section. Much like traditional labor, a lot can happen in those few hours. In general, if you have babies that are pointed down in the correct position, a vaginal delivery is probably going to be possible. It depends on your own comfort level and your doctor's recommendation whether or not you try to deliver vaginally or just schedule a C-section. Sometimes, one baby can be in the perfect position for a vaginal delivery, yet the second baby could be facing the wrong way. This is to be expected of twins since they are two different babies. There is a lot of moving around that can happen during the last few months of your pregnancy.

There are some instances where the mother can deliver one baby vaginally, yet needs to have a C-section for the second baby. This is not uncommon, and if it is in your babies' best interest, then your doctor is going to let you know if this should be the birth plan for you.

Every step of the way, your doctor is going to be keeping you updated and provide you with recommendations on what they believe is the most successful decision to make during delivery. This is why it is important to always keep an open mind about your birth plan; it can change in an instant.

Keep in mind that both babies aren't always going to be ready to come out at the same time. When you go into labor, this might only be triggered by one of the babies. Your water could break, just as it would in a traditional pregnancy, and you might give birth to your first child. Then, the waiting begins. Normally, one baby is always going to be ready sooner than the other. This is why mothers who are expecting twins can have a different type of labor; it can almost feel like double labor. If your second baby takes minutes, or even hours, to finally be ready to come out, you are going to have to endure even more anticipation and waiting.

You will actually be giving birth in an operating room just in case either of the babies needs additional assistance during delivery. You can expect to be accompanied by your partner, any loved ones you invite into the room, your doctor, one nurse for each baby, and neonatal intensive care doctors standing by. While this might seem overwhelming, this is necessary because of how different delivering twins as compared to delivering a single baby. Know that every single person present is there to support you and help you. They want what is best for you, and no one is going to be judging you or pressuring you to deliver your babies in a certain way. The only time recommendations are going to be made is when they will clearly benefit your babies.

Homebirth is not recommended for twins because of all the complexities that can happen during your delivery. While a lot of women dream of having a home birth, this just isn't exactly going to be a reality when you are having more than one baby at a time. Waterbirth in a hospital is still an option, though. If you do want to experience the comfort of having a water birth, discuss this with your doctor early on. They can have everything set up for you in the room, but know that you might have to be moved back onto a hospital bed if you do need to undergo a C-section or any other procedure during the delivery. The hospital is always going to try to accommodate your requests and desires because they know this can be a very special, yet stressful, time for the expecting mother.

Remember that your partner is also going to be handling a rollercoaster ride of emotions. Though they will not be giving birth, they are going to be supporting you in every way they can. Whether it be distracting you or holding your hand during any painful moments, your partner will also be under a lot of excitement and anxiety at the same time. It can almost feel like they are helpless when they are there with you as you work through your labor. Do your best to show your appreciation for them, even if it means a simple hand squeeze from time to time to reassure them that they are a part of this process too.

Chapter 10: Dad's Role

It is talked about less often, but the dad's role throughout pregnancy and delivery is an extremely important one. Your partner is in this with you, and this is their child too. Just because they did not get to feel any of the morning sickness or baby kicks does not mean that they aren't just as invested as you are in the whole process. This chapter will focus on what the dad's role is and how to work through certain feelings that arise or questions that come up. There is a myth that tends to circulate that a dad does not have to do much at all when a mother is pregnant, but that is not even close to the truth. Not only is the dad going to be the main support system, but he is also going to be learning and discovering just as the mother will.

The Importance

Feelings of cluelessness are normal for first-time dads. This is a brand new experience, and it should not be expected of every dad to know exactly what to do and when to do it. Just as the mother is going to be dealing with different changes, the father will also have to do the same thing. The main way to be a helpful father to an expecting mother is to just be there for her. Accompanying her to all of her doctor appointments is the first step. This will provide her with a sense of support, and you will also get to experience all of the same news and information that she will experience.

Try to do some research on your own time. The more you can learn about pregnancy and delivery is going to help your partner. Just as her own education on her pregnancy is valuable, your education is deemed just as valuable. Taking initiative is what makes you a great father from the very beginning. When it comes to picking out names, participate in the process! This is your chance to make a decision with your significant other. Think about the names that you like and make suggestions when the mother decides that she would like to talk about what you would like to name your new baby.

Doing housework is a great way to be helpful to an expecting mother. As her pregnancy progresses, she isn't going to be able to do all of the chores that she usually does. All of the bending down and walking around that can be avoided will help to put her body at ease. Communicate with her every chance you get. If she isn't feeling well, ask her directly what you can do for her that would help. A significant other that is willing to ask is a lot better than one who simply stands on the sidelines and waits for instructions.

What to Expect

In the beginning, you aren't going to notice that many changes. The expectant mother might feel sick more often than usual, but you can help by ensuring that she stays hydrated and well-nourished. Remind her to take her prenatal vitamins, and cook nutritious meals for her when she is hungry. In the first trimester, you shouldn't have to change much about your typical routine as a couple. The symptoms that she will be dealing with should be manageable, and if they aren't, you can take her to the doctor to see if there are any solutions that will make them easier to handle.

As the pregnancy progresses, the expecting mother is going to reach a point where she might stop working and stop driving. This is where you are going to have to pick up the slack. You will be the one driving her to her appointments, running errands, and going anywhere else that you need to go. Whether it is late-night runs to the supermarket for food or trips to the pharmacy to pick up medication, you can expect to be doing it all. This is the point where it will usually become more tiring for you. Again, if you are prepared for all of this, there is no reason for you to become stressed out at the thought of it.

When the birth plan is being created, you should have a say in this, too. While the expecting mother is going to have her own preferences, she will likely be asking you what you think about her choices. Be honest with her, and offer any helpful advice that you feel will make the labor and delivery easier. If a home birth or water birth is scheduled, do your best to make sure that everything is going to be in place when the time comes. Being a great father begins with being a great planner; think about every detail.

How to Help

Do not tell her what to do. No matter what you are communicating about, an expecting mother does not particularly need to be told what to do regarding her own body and how she is feeling. While you might have great ideas, you can bring these up to her, but don't be offended if she decides that something else is going to be better for her. Remember, you can't feel exactly what she is feeling. Being there for support and to bounce ideas off of is extremely helpful, but being bossy or controlling is not. You need to let her take the lead when it comes to her pregnancy.

Be there to listen to her. There will be times when she simply wants to vent or complain about her symptoms. Let her do this. While there might be nothing she can do but wait them out, at least she can have you there as a support system who will always lend a listening ear. She might ask you for advice if she is unsure of things and this will bring you even closer together as a couple. Each decision that the two of you make together is going to impact your baby. While you might not know exactly what you are doing if it is your first time, let those instincts kick in.

Take her shopping for baby items. Once the first trimester is over and people have been told that you are expecting a little bundle of joy, a lot of the fun can begin. Most couples create a baby registry at a store of their choosing. Aside from these items that will be given as gifts, there are still plenty of things that the parents will have to purchase as they prepare for the arrival of their child. Going shopping for these things really solidifies the idea that your baby is going to be there soon. Do things for the baby's nursery, as well. Being able to decorate and design the nursery together is a great bonding experience.

Identifying Feelings

As a soon-to-be-father, you are going to have so many emotions running through your mind and heart. While the mother usually gets to express herself more frequently, know that all of your emotions are also valid. You might be worried about how you are going to care for the baby because you are unfamiliar with what to do, but you also might be incredibly excited to mold a young mind with your own morals, values, and traditions. No matter what the case is, express yourself! The expecting mother will appreciate that she isn't alone with any of her feelings. Fathers can often take a back seat to the point where it might seem like they don't have any strong emotions, but that isn't always true.

You are about to take on several new responsibilities, all in a short matter of time. Just as the mother might have some things to change about her lifestyle when she finds out she is pregnant, so will the father. For example, if you enjoy going out on the weekends with your friends, you might need to spend more time at home as the expecting mother experiences more intense symptoms. While you cannot tell what it is like to physically feel these things, you can definitely support her as she goes through them. If any feelings come up that are overwhelming (either positive or negative), talk to her about them. She will appreciate your openness. You don't need to pretend that you know exactly what is going to happen because let's face it, you both probably don't. Pregnancy is a learning experience that you will work through together.

Sex during Pregnancy

The only reason to avoid sex during pregnancy is if either of you is not in the mood to have it. There is nothing that you will do to hurt the baby while you are having sex; that is just a myth. Feel free to be intimate with one another, and know that your baby is still going to be growing and developing just fine. If you do want to take some extra precautions, know that your partner's breasts are likely going to be more tender than usual. Any grabbing or squeezing might feel more intense than usual, so keep that in mind. Of course, if she expresses that there is any pain, you should stop immediately. Otherwise, feel free to have as much sex as you both want to, intercourse included.

A lot of couples find that the pregnancy hormones actually do a lot for the woman's arousal. She might feel extra willing and able to have sex in the beginning. As her belly begins to grow, you might have to find some new positions that allow you both to be comfortable because anything that involves her bending forward or being on her stomach for too long will understandably be uncomfortable. Much like the sleeping position, if she can lie down on her left side while you position yourself behind her, much like spooning, this tends to be a very comfortable and pleasurable position for couples who are expecting.

Consider that she might be more emotional than usual. Do your best to incorporate a lot of foreplay before you begin having sex. If you are too rough, this can be off-putting to a woman who is currently producing high amounts of hormones that make her feel more tender and loving than usual. Allow her to be the center of attention, and ask her what feels good. Communication does not have to be a mood-killer; it will actually help you become better lovers.

Overcoming Intimacy Issues

Even though she is in the mood, you might have trouble getting into the mood yourself. This is okay, and this is normal. Pregnancy changes a lot. It forces you to think a lot more responsibly and practically than you would have before. There is also the issue of you feeling that you are going to hurt the expecting mother if you advance in any type of intimate way. Rest assured that she will be able to tell you if something hurts or if it is uncomfortable. A lot of pregnant women regularly have and enjoy sex throughout their pregnancy with no problems, physically or emotionally.

Understandably, there might still be a few things that you are worried that you will have to work through. Talk to her about your feelings, just as mentioned earlier. Working together, you can overcome any worries that you might have in order to get back to the core of your intimacy. Starting with simple touching and massage, these acts of intimacy can go a long way and allow you to start having sex again. She is going to appreciate all of the little things you do for her, even if they are not sexual. Opening doors for her and cooking her meals are little and intimate ways to show her that you care.

A Dad's Role during Delivery

Early Labor

As the woman enters early labor, your main job is to be her distraction. She is going to be feeling contractions, and these are uncomfortable. Do your best to take her mind off of them, but do not make her feel ignored. If she needs to complain, be her ear to listen. Read to her, talk about some of your favorite things, bring up funny memories, and do anything you can to get her mind focused on something else. If she stays too focused on the pain, her active labor is going to feel even worse. Try to get her up and moving. Walking around can alleviate a lot more pain than simply staying still. Walk her up and down the hallways if she feels like she can.

Active Labor

As you know from any classes you have taken or any research you have done, active labor means more active contractions. They are going to

196

become stronger and closer together, and at this point, you will likely need to provide your hand for her to squeeze. Rub her back and reassure her that she is doing a great job. If you notice that she is starting to panic, try your best to get her back to a calm state of mind. Just as you learned in class, you are going to be her support system during this time. Try to work on breathing techniques that you have learned. Know that she is naturally going to be agitated and moody during this point. Allow her to have this moment because you don't know what she's feeling. She might be snappy, but know that she is definitely appreciating the little things you are doing for her.

Delivery

The moment has come - the baby is on its way! This part happens very quickly sometimes, and it can be hard to absorb everything that is going on. The most important thing that you can do here is to remain calm. If you are calm, then she is going to know that things are okay. The instant you lose your cool, she is going to feel panicked. If she is delivering vaginally, you can hold her hand and motivate her as she pushes. Encourage her to keep going and that it is almost over. In a C-section, she isn't going to be able to feel and see as much, so you can be her eyes. If she wants to know what is going on, you can describe it to her.

A Dad's Role after Delivery

There are normally two impulses that you will feel after your baby is born - you will want to cry and you will want to take photos. Both are completely valid reactions, as a miracle has just occurred. Be mindful that the mother has gone through so much to get to this point, and while she is definitely going to appreciate having pictures of the moment, she might not want a camera in her face for too long. Take a few shots, and then put the camera down so you can meet your baby together. If your baby is considered at-risk, then the baby will likely be taken to the nursery shortly after delivery so the mother can rest and the baby can be monitored. You can alternate between visiting with your child and keeping the mother company. If the baby is not at risk, the mother will be handed her child directly after giving birth.

In between all of this, you can make phone calls to inform your loved ones that the baby has finally arrived. It is going to be a surreal and joyous moment that you will never forget. When you go back to visit your partner, let her know how well the baby is doing, and also be sure to mention how amazing she was at delivering your little bundle of joy. She might still be in shock from the entire process, but keeping her calm and reassured is what will bring her back down to a calm state of being.

Some mothers who have to deviate from their birth plan might feel a little upset at this point, and if this has happened in your case, remind her that it was what needed to be done to have a healthy baby. If you tell her how great the baby is doing and that all of the right decisions were made, she will eventually get over not having the exact birth plan of her choosing. It can naturally be a very overwhelming time, and at the moment, it might feel like the doctors were making all of the decisions. Reassure her that you were there every step of the way and that you agreed with all of the decisions that were made. It will help her to know that you were looking out for her body and for your baby. From this moment on, the mother should feel your love. Make it a point that you are going to love her in every single moment, from childbirth to simply being together at home. Loving her always is how you are going to keep your own personal bond as strong as new parents.

Chapter 11: Postpartum

The intense part is over - you have a baby now! All of the anticipation and hours of labor have likely all melted away the instant you set your eyes on your newborn baby. This is when all of the real fun begins. You are now responsible for raising a child, and you are going to continue to learn even more about being a parent. While you are doing all of this, you are also going to be simultaneously recovering both physically and emotionally. This chapter is going to breakdown everything you need to know about your postpartum stage and what is to be expected.

The First Week

What You Are Feeling

After you have your baby, you are going to be feeling a whirlwind of emotions. Surprisingly, not all of these emotions are going to be cheerful and happy. Remember, you have just gone through nearly a year of carrying a developing baby, only to end up delivering it and then eventually caring for it. This is a lot of pressure that is put on you as a mother, and while you have a partner who is willing to support you, there are some things that your partner did not have the chance to experience along with you. These are some of the feelings that most mothers do not realize can occur after giving birth:

1. Sadness: Yes, it is normal to feel sad after you give birth. There are a few reasons why this might happen. Postpartum depression is a very real condition that a lot of mothers experience. Even when you are overjoyed that you have a brand new baby, the depression can still set in. Talk to your doctor if you believe you are experiencing this depression. Some sadness can be because you are no longer pregnant, and you have become so used to being pregnant. Even though you have your baby in your arms now, not having

your baby in your belly shows just how fast their childhood can go.

2. Fear: Getting home from the hospital and being alone as a family, your first instinct might be to freak out. You've never done this before; it is natural to be scared. The thing about parenting is that you are going to learn as you go. Just because you might not have it all figured out right now does not mean that you can't learn. Sure, you might make mistakes, but every single parent does.

3. Anxiety: When you bring your baby home, it might feel impossible for you to relax. You are constantly going to be checking on your little one to see if they need anything. Don't let yourself get too jittery. Remember, you are in recovery at this point. You can only do so much, plus, you have a partner who is willing to help you. Let him help!

What You Are Wondering

You are likely trying to decipher what your baby is thinking and feeling. All your baby can do right now is cry, become fussy, and sleep, so you might be left wondering how in the world you are supposed to know what to do next. Your motherly instinct is going to kick in. A newborn baby normally only needs a few things: feeding, sleep, a clean diaper, and rocking/cuddling. If one of these doesn't seem to soothe your baby, try another. This process is definitely going to involve a lot of trial and error, whether other parents ever admit it or not.

Your first week home is your chance to form a routine. Newborn babies usually eat around every 2-3 hours, so you can time any diaper changes based on this feeding schedule. Your baby is likely going to sleep a lot, and you might be very tempted to wake them up so you can play. Avoid doing so because their body is still adjusting to being outside of the womb. Things feel different for them too, so they need to do their own form of regulation. You are going to be up and down throughout the night, but that is to be expected.

Some babies are great sleepers; others can't stay asleep for more than an hour at a time. You will find out how well your baby sleeps right away. There isn't too much you can do for your baby if they are simply fussy. This will get better as the baby grows older, but for now, you just need to keep checking on them and ensuring that everything is as comfortable as possible where the baby is sleeping. Try putting your baby down to sleep after they are fed and burped. When they are full, they are more likely to feel comfortable enough to stay asleep for a longer period of time.

The Beginning of Breastfeeding

The first few days after your baby is born, your body will generally produce enough milk for you on its own. It is milk that is rich in nutrients that your baby needs. It is normal for your breasts to feel firmer within the first 3-4 days after producing this milk. Even if your body takes a little bit longer to produce the milk, this is perfectly normal because every woman is different. If you are able, begin breastfeeding a few hours after your baby is born. When you are still in the hospital, the nurses will be there to assist you with getting your baby to latch properly.

If you intend on breastfeeding exclusively, then it is wise to avoid giving your baby a bottle or pacifier because this can cause confusion when it comes to latching. Being able to latch onto your breast is going to be a different feeling than latching onto an artificial nipple or pacifier. To get your baby to begin feeding, simply hold them in your arms and place their mouth near your breast. They will normally have the natural instinct to latch on and begin eating.

Once you get home from the hospital, you will have to keep an eye on the signs of hunger. These include when your baby moves their head from side to side when their mouth opens, if their mouth starts to pucker, or if they begin to nuzzle against your chest. The more you breastfeed, the more familiar you will become with these signs. If your baby is acting particularly fussy, you can try getting them to latch on because it could also mean that they are hungry or need the comfort of being latched to the mother. You might need to guide your nipple into your baby's mouth by supporting your breast with one hand and positioning your baby with the other. If your baby begins to suck without getting much milk, this is an indication that they are not properly latched on. Try again, and remember, this part is going to take practice from both of you.

Expert Sleep Strategies for Newborns

1. Be Aware of Light: If you are putting your baby down for a nap during the day, you will want the room to be dim but not fully dark. Any bright lighting is simply going

to tell your baby that it is "go" time, and they will be more likely to want to stay awake.

2. Put Your Baby Down When They Are Drowsy: If you wait until your baby is fully asleep, setting them down in the crib might create the exact opposite effect than what you are trying to accomplish. This sudden change can wake your baby. Try to place your baby down when they are drowsy and just about to fall asleep. Timing is everything for this strategy.

3. Give Them Time to Self-Soothe: If your baby is asleep in the crib, they are going to naturally stir and make noise from time to time. Before running into the nursery, allow your baby time to get comfortable again because a lot of the time, a baby is able to self-soothe and go back to sleep.

4. Avoid Eye Contact: It sounds funny, but if you are trying to put your baby to sleep, avoid making direct eye contact. This can

be engaging in a newborn, and it might cause them to want to stay awake longer. Whether you are rocking your baby in your arms or in a rocker, try to keep your gaze neutral and not directly on the baby.

5. Feed Your Baby Late at Night: While this will sometimes happen inevitably, it is a good idea to semi-wake your baby between 10 PM and 12 AM for a feeding. This will allow them to stay full and comfortable while also promoting longer stretches of sleep so you and your partner also get the chance to rest through the night.

6. Be Relaxed on Diaper Changing Schedules: It might be tempting to change your baby each time they wake up, but sometimes, waking up does not mean that your baby is ready to stay awake. It is important to learn your baby's wet diaper schedule in order to see if they are getting enough food. Definitely monitor this for the purpose of the baby's health, but if

you do pick them up to change them every time, this could actually be disrupting their developing sleep schedule. Using moderation is the key here. Make sure that you put on a heavy-duty diaper before your baby is going to sleep for a longer period of time.

The First Six Weeks

What You Are Feeling

At this point, you might be experiencing what is known as perineum soreness. This can happen because a lot of women tear in this area if they give birth vaginally. Your perineum is the skin between your vagina and anus. Even if you did not tear, you likely still experienced pressure there during the delivery, so you might feel some pain. Afterbirth pains are also fairly common during this time. These will feel like standard belly cramps, and they happen because the uterus is shrinking back down to its original size.

If you had a C-section, it is common for your incision to feel a bit sore, as well.

To ease any of the postpartum pain mentioned above, you can perform Kegel exercises to strengthen your pelvic floor muscles. You can also place an ice pack on your perineum to directly ease some of the pain. Sitting in a warm, shallow bath is also great to ease any type of vaginal or abdominal discomfort. You can add sea salt to cleanse yourself and your bathwater. If the pain does not subside on its own, you can ask your doctor for more options or medications to assist you.

Vaginal discharge is normal during this time. Even after your baby is born, your uterus is still trying to get rid of certain tissue and blood inside of your body. The discharge will look like period blood, and it might even include some blood clots. Over time, your flow will get lighter. You can wear period pads until this subsides. It can last for a few weeks or even a month after you give birth.

What You Are Wondering

If you begin sweating a lot more after giving birth, this is normal. It tends to happen especially at night, and it is caused by all of the hormones that your body has created during the pregnancy. You might also be wondering why you are still so tired after you have given birth. Even though you are not physically carrying your baby inside of you anymore, you are caring for your baby at every hour, day and night. Do your best to sleep when your baby sleeps so you can preserve as much of your energy as possible. Don't be afraid to ask for help! Let your partner soothe the baby, and let any loved ones come over and help if they offer. Their help will allow you the time to rest.

Another burning question is when you are going to lose your baby weight. Immediately after giving birth, you should lose around 10lbs. In the next few weeks, you will also naturally begin to lose weight. To get your body toned and back to its original state before you became pregnant, staying active and eating healthy are the best ways to do this. There is no secret to dropping the pounds overnight, and you do not have to immediately get back into the gym and workout for hours a day. Simply get up and moving. Taking walks and doing low-impact exercises like yoga and Pilates can help you. Also, keep in mind that what you eat still matters because you are breastfeeding. Even if you are not in a rush to lose any weight at all, your baby is still receiving nutrients from the foods that you eat.

Physical and Emotional Changes

Your body is going to look different after you give birth; every woman experiences this. You might have stretch marks that you didn't have prior to your pregnancy. The skin around your belly might be loose. Remember that you just gave birth to a healthy baby that you spent 9 months growing inside of you. This is a lot for your body to handle, so yes, things are going to look different. This doesn't mean that they will look different forever, though. Try not to be so hard on yourself or compare your body to any other postpartum body that you've seen. Your metabolism is unique, so it is going to take some time for you to get back to your original appearance. If you can help it, try to overlook these changes and remind yourself that you have a beautiful baby now.

Emotionally, you can be going through a lot at this point. There will be times of pure exhaustion because of all the broken sleep you are getting. There will also be times of elation and joy as you watch your baby grow and learn. It can be overwhelming with just how many feelings you can go through in a day. There is also the possibility that you can develop postpartum depression, as mentioned earlier in the guide. If you ever feel that you cannot handle your emotions, or if you believe that something does not feel right, consult your doctor.

Getting Back Into Shape

As mentioned, when you feel ready to get back into your pre-pregnancy body, go for it! There is no rush to get there by a certain deadline, though. Do what feels right to you. Low-impact exercises that focus on building up core strength are the best for getting your belly flat. When you were pregnant, there were certain muscles that you had to avoid putting a strain on for the safety of the baby. Now that you have this freedom again, work your way into exercising slowly. If you overdo it in the beginning because you are eager to get back into shape, you could end up hurting yourself and setting yourself back for even more weeks.

Create a realistic workout routine for yourself that includes exercises that are appropriate for how your body currently feels and for the free time that you have. Make an arrangement with your partner for 30 minutes to an hour where he will commit to taking care of the baby so you can get this done. As long as you are willing to stick to a routine, you will be able to get back into shape fairly easily. All it takes is the commitment to taking care of yourself.

Reasons to Do This Again Someday

After all that you have been through, you might feel that you don't want to have any more kids. This is valid, and a lot of women make this decision because of what they had to go through during pregnancy and delivery. On the other hand, even despite all of the pain and hard work, many women feel that pregnancy is worth it every single time. If you want to put your body through it again, have as many children as you and your partner desire!

If you want your baby to have siblings, this can also be a reason to consider having more kids in the future. Having 2 young babies at once can be difficult, but if you wait a few years, you might feel keener on having another child in order for your firstborn to have a little brother or sister. No matter what you decide to do, know that

216

there is no pressure to ever have another child again. The decision is a personal one, and it is solely up to you and your partner.

Conclusion

Having a baby is something that you will never forget. There is no other experience like it, and this is why so many people consider childbirth to be such a miraculous process. After growing your baby inside of you for so long, the bond that you have as soon as that child is born already exists and is as strong as can be. Raising a child is hard work, and after going through an entire pregnancy and delivery, you will likely have a newfound appreciation for all of the mothers that you have ever known.

As you go through each trimester of your pregnancy, the main thing you need to realize is that you are not going to be alone. With the support of your partner and the wisdom of your team of doctors and nurses, all of your questions and concerns are going to be handled. Each thing that changes in your body will be felt and explained if you feel that you need an explanation. When you begin to experience your first round of pregnancy symptoms, know that there is always something that you can do to alleviate them. Having pregnancy symptoms is a sign that your baby is developing as it should. While it can be rough on you, know that these symptoms are happening for a reason.

Not every pregnancy is going to look exactly alike. You might start showing right away or you might barely even show at all. Don't compare yourself to anyone else because this is your baby and your body. Know that you always have choices, from what happens during your birth plan to what you'd like your doctor to test your baby for while it is still in the womb. Ultimately, you become a mother as soon as you get the confirmation from your doctor that you are pregnant. That motherly instinct kicks in a lot faster than you think.

As promised, this book was made for the purpose of providing you with reassurance. You are a strong and capable woman, and your body knows exactly what to do in order to develop and deliver a healthy baby. With the tips on how to ease your sickness and ailments, you will be able to get through each trimester like a champ. By understanding how to work with your partner and communicate during each step, you will both feel included in the process of pregnancy and the delivery alike. When you know what to expect at each doctor's appointment and in the delivery room, you will be able to enter each situation with the confidence that you need in order to get through it. The sooner that you are able to endure all that comes with your pregnancy, the sooner you get to meet your wonderful new addition to the family.

The moment that you discover you are pregnant, this book is made to guide you through every step of the way so that you do not feel scared. Instead of wondering about the worst things that can happen to your body or the baby, you should be looking forward to the positive things instead. This guide should inform and educate you on topics that you are going to encounter as you experience your pregnancy journey. You will understand why it is a journey as you realize things about yourself and your body that you likely didn't even know was possible before. A woman's body is incredibly resilient and tough; most people do not give it enough credit. When you can recognize that in yourself, it is something to feel proud of.

No matter what decisions you make during your pregnancy, know that you are doing what is best for you. Without the influence of anyone else, you should have an idea of what you want for your baby, your body, and your family. This is what being a mother is all about. By learning how to accept these ideas that you come up with and have the confidence in yourself to make them happen, you are already being the best mother you can be. Never forget that childbirth is not something that simply happens on its own. A successful birth story is a combination of a healthy baby and a mother's strong will to do her very best.

Hello there Soon to be Mom,

Having a baby is one of the most exciting and life-changing experiences you can have. You've probably dreamed of many of the special moments you'll have with your new baby, but have you thought about how you want to actually give birth to your little bundle of joy? It's important to contemplate and make note of your vision for giving birth in a birth plan

"Make preparations in advance. You will never have trouble if you are prepared for it." - Theodore Roosevelt

You can never be totally in charge of your labor and delivery (childbirth is generally a pretty out of control thing), but a birth plan ensures that you and your partner are on the same page as your doctors and nurses when it comes to issues like pain meds, people allowed in the delivery room, episiotomies, cord cutting, etc.

So, don´t wait longer to receive "Your Personal Birth Plan Checklist Guide" in PDF format by typing the link below or scan the QR code with your mobile phone:

https://harleycarrparenting.com/worry-free-pregnancy

OR

Print the document and fill out the checklist box according to your choices.

Use this easy fill-in-the-blank birth plan to prepare yourself for delivery and communicate your wants and needs to your medical team. Now, you can have your Birth Plan in just a minute!

Enjoy and Best Wishes to you Mommy!

Harley Carr

References

3 weeks pregnant - Pregnancy symptoms week 3. (2019, October 8). Retrieved November 13, 2019, from https://www.whattoexpect.com/pregnancy/week-by-week/week-3.aspx

Baby Centre Medical Advisory Board. (2005, April 21). What to pack in your hospital bag: Your complete checklist. Retrieved November 13, 2019, from https://www.babycentre.co.uk/what-to-pack-in-your-hospital-bag

Barllaro, M. (2019). 7 post-pregnancy feelings no one warns you about. Retrieved November 13, 2019, from https://www.parents.com/baby/new-parent/emotions/7-post-pregnancy-feelings-no-one-warns-you-about/

Bed Rest. (2019). Retrieved November 12, 2019, from

https://americanpregnancy.org/pregnancy-complications/bed-rest/

Ben-Joseph, E. (2018). Breastfeeding FAQs: Getting started (for parents) - KidsHealth. Retrieved November 13, 2019, from https://kidshealth.org/en/parents/breastfeed-starting.html

Carey, E. (2015, August 5). Having twins? Here's what you need to know. Retrieved November 13, 2019, from https://www.healthline.com/health/pregnancy/having-twins-what-to-expect#Delivery

Cherney, K. (2019, April 5). Natural vs. Epidural: What to expect. Retrieved November 13, 2019, from https://www.healthline.com/health/pregnancy/natural-birth-vs-epidural#using-an-epidural

Daly, K., & Reece, T. (2019). Pregnancy weight gain: What to expect and why it's not as bad as you think. Retrieved November 13, 2019,

from
https://www.parents.com/pregnancy/my-body/weight-gain/why-pregnancy-weight-gain-isnt-as-bad-as-you-think/

Diet during pregnancy. (2019). Retrieved November 12, 2019, from https://americanpregnancy.org/pregnancy-health/diet-during-pregnancy

Ding, K. (2019, October 29). Expert sleep strategies for babies. Retrieved November 13, 2019, from https://www.babycenter.com/0_expert-sleep-strategies-for-babies_1445907.bc

Drelsbach, S. (2019). Top 14 pregnancy fears (and why you shouldn't worry). Retrieved November 13, 2019, from https://www.parents.com/pregnancy/complications/health-and-safety-issues/top-pregnancy-fears/

Eating seafood during pregnancy. (2019). Retrieved November 12, 2019, from

https://americanpregnancy.org/pregnancy-
health/eating-seafood-during-pregnancy

Fuentes, A. (2018). Prenatal tests: FAQs (for
parents) - KidsHealth. Retrieved November
13, 2019, from
https://kidshealth.org/en/parents/prenatal-
tests.html

Getting sick while pregnant. (2019). Retrieved
November 12, 2019, from
https://americanpregnancy.org/pregnancy-
complications/sick-while-pregnant

Johnson, T. (2018, July 2). How much vitamin
B6 should you get when you're pregnant?
Retrieved November 13, 2019, from
https://www.webmd.com/baby/qa/how-
much-vitamin-b6-should-you-get-when-
youre-pregnant

Khan, A. (2018, September 19). 21 common
pregnancy problems and their solutions.
Retrieved November 13, 2019, from
https://parenting.firstcry.com/articles/21-

common-pregnancy-problems-and-their-
solutions/

Lucla, C. A., Hartshorn, J. (n. d.) The benefits of
breastfeeding. Retrieved November 12, 2019,
from
https://www.parents.com/baby/breastfeedin
g/basics/the-benefits-of-breastfeeding

Mann, D. (2008, June 3). 11 things you didn't
know about twin pregnancies. Retrieved
November 13, 2019, from
https://www.webmd.com/baby/features/11-
things-you-didnt-know-about-twin-
pregnancies#4

Marcin, A. (2018, July 10). Waterbirth pros and
cons: Is it right for you? Retrieved November
13, 2019, from
https://www.healthline.com/health/pregnan
cy/water-birth#risks

Marcin, A. (2018, September 14). What
medicines can I take while pregnant?
Retrieved November 13, 2019, from

https://www.healthline.com/health/pregnancy/what-medicines-are-safe-during-pregnancy

Marple, K. (2019, November 1). How to choose an obstetrician. Retrieved November 13, 2019, from https://www.babycenter.com/0_how-to-choose-an-obstetrician_1582.bc

National Sleep Foundation. (2019). Pregnancy & sleep - national sleep foundation. Retrieved November 13, 2019, from https://www.sleepfoundation.org/articles/pregnancy-and-sleep

Nierenberg, C. (2017, June 17). C-section: Procedure & recovery. Retrieved November 13, 2019, from https://www.livescience.com/44726-c-section.html

Nierenberg, C. (2018, March 27). Vaginal birth vs. C-section: Pros & cons. Retrieved November 13, 2019, from https://www.livescience.com/45681-vaginal-birth-vs-c-section.html

Pampers. (2018, July 5). Learn the signs of labour from Pampers PH. Retrieved November 13, 2019, from https://www.pampers.ph/pregnancy/pregnancy-symptoms/article/signs-of-labour-how-to-read-your-bodys-signals?gclid=CjwKCAjwlovtBRBrEiwAG3XJ-yagbXRHppq8WnF2VSZoP_vMpl-c5qyR0k7yoz5tgfDe9m336q2P-xoC-R0QAvD_BwE&gclsrc=aw.ds

Parents. (2019). 11 ways to ease contractions without drugs. Retrieved November 13, 2019, from https://www.parents.com/pregnancy/giving-birth/labor-and-delivery/10-ways-to-ease-contractions-without-drugs/

Pillai, S. (2014, December 19). 5 reasons why it is unsafe to have deli meats in pregnancy. Retrieved November 13, 2019, from https://www.momjunction.com/articles/is-

it-safe-to-eat-deli-meats-during-
pregnancy_00118527/#gref

Reading labels. (2015, December 2). Retrieved
November 13, 2019, from
https://www.allinahealth.org/health-
conditions-and-treatments/health-
library/patient-education/beginnings/diet-
and-exercise/reading-labels

Smith, S. (2018, June 7). The important role of
fathers during pregnancy. Retrieved
November 13, 2019, from
https://www.marriage.com/advice/pregnanc
y/the-important-role-of-fathers-during-
pregnancy/

Surviving pregnancy without your favorite vices.
(2017, December 15). Retrieved November
13, 2019, from
https://carepointhealth.org/surviving-
pregnancy-without-favorite-vices/

Symptoms of pregnancy: What happens first.
(2019, May 11). Retrieved November 13,

2019, from
https://www.mayoclinic.org/healthy-lifestyle/getting-pregnant/in-depth/symptoms-of-pregnancy/art-20043853

Three vices that need to be dropped pre, post, and during pregnancy. (2019). Retrieved November 12, 2019, from https://www.babyandme.com/three-vices-that-need-to-be-dropped-pre-post-and-during-pregnancy

Travel during pregnancy - ACOG. (2019). Retrieved November 12, 2019, from https://www.acog.org/Patients/FAQs/Travel-During-Pregnancy?IsMobileSet=falseWorking

Types of prenatal vitamins. (2019). Retrieved November 12, 2019, from https://americanpregnancy.org/pregnancy-health/types-prenatal-vitamins/

Vitamin D and pregnancy. (2019). Retrieved

November 12, 2019, from
https://americanpregnancy.org/pregnancy-health/vitamin-d-and-pregnancy/

Wikipedia contributors. (2019, October 14). Maternity leave in the United States. Retrieved November 13, 2019, from https://en.wikipedia.org/wiki/Maternity_leave_in_the_United_States

Woolston, C. (2019, January 1). Dad's role in the delivery room. Retrieved November 13, 2019, from https://consumer.healthday.com/encyclopedia/emotional-health-17/love-sex-and-relationship-health-news-452/dad-s-role-in-the-delivery-room-643267.html

Your body after baby: The first 6 weeks. (2018). Retrieved November 13, 2019, from https://www.marchofdimes.org/pregnancy/your-body-after-baby-the-first-6-weeks.aspx

Your first prenatal visit. (2019). Retrieved November 12, 2019, from https://americanpregnancy.org/planning/first-prenatal-visit/

Made in the USA
Monee, IL
09 September 2020

41751171R00142